*Camping
Out in the
Yellowstone
1882*

✒ Camping Out in the Yellowstone 1882

Mary Bradshaw Richards

EDITED BY
William W. Slaughter

University of Utah Press
Salt Lake City

Map by Thomas Child

CATALOGING IN PUBLICATION DATA

Richards, Mary Bradshaw, b. 1825.
    Camping out in the Yellowstone, 1882 / Mary Bradshaw
Richards ; edited by William W. Slaughter.
        p.   cm.
    Originally appeared as eleven articles in the Salem observer.
    ISBN 0-87480-449-3 (paper : acid-free paper)
    1. Yellowstone National Park. 2. Camping—Yellowstone
National Park—History—19th century, I. Slaughter,
William W., 1952–
II. Title.
F722.R515 1994
796.54'09787'52—dc20
                                        93-46135

To my parents,

Evelyn O. Slaughter and Solomon W. Slaughter
who first took me to Yellowstone,

and to all who love Yellowstone:

"What would the world be, once bereft
Of wet and of wildness? Let them be left,
O let them be left, wildness and wet;
Long live the weeds and the wilderness yet."
—Gerard Manley Hopkins (1881)

CONTENTS

INTRODUCTION

In the summer of 1882 Mary Bradshaw Richards and her husband, Jesse Mayne Richards, traveled to Yellowstone National Park from their home in New York City.[1] They were not a young couple; she was 57 years old and he would be 54 come October. They journeyed not as VIPs or as hardened western explorers but as mature and experienced tourists who were eager to see America's new "Wonderland." Mary captured what she saw and felt in a series of letters to the *Salem Observer* of Massachusetts. The timing of their trip is significant because it occurred in the transitional period after Yellowstone was a truly "out-back and beyond" experience and before the park began to be developed with improved roads, hotels, and services.

1. "Hotel Arrivals," *The Salt Lake Daily Tribune* (28 July 1882): 4. The list stated that "J. M. Richards and wife, New York" were registered at the Continental Hotel.

The America the Richards traveled through in 1882 was a place of change intermixed with traditional ways. Chester A. Arthur was the nation's twenty-first president. The first Labor Day was celebrated that year as 30,000 workers marched in New York City. Congress passed the Chinese Exclusion Act, which created a ten-year ban on Chinese immigration into the United States. Distinguished literary figures Henry Wadsworth Longfellow and Ralph Waldo Emerson died within a month of each other; and Jesse James was murdered by Robert Ford. Future president Franklin D. Roosevelt was born. In Appleton, Wisconsin, the first hydroelectric plant was built.

In the East, John D. Rockefeller created the first "trust" when he formed the Standard Oil Company. Mark Twain's *The Prince and the Pauper* was published. New York City caught "Langtry fever" as the stunning actress Lillie Langtry made her debut on the American stage. The world's first electrically lighted Christmas tree was introduced in New York.

In the West, many of the ranchlands and farmlands were plagued by drought. The Cowboy was beginning to pass into legend as the era of the long trail drive gave way to barbed wire and big business, but twenty-two-year-old Butch Cassidy was just establishing himself as a famed outlaw. The Mormons were worrying about the consequences of the newly enacted Edmunds anti-polygamy law. And Yellowstone National Park was ten years old, still wild and full of wonders. In order to appreciate the Richards' journey to this magical land, it is helpful to take a look at its history.

For centuries Native Americans had lived, hunted, fished, made arrowheads, and found lodge poles in the Yellowstone area. The Crows to the east of the park, the Shoshones to the south, the Blackfeet to the north, and the Bannocks to the west occasionally traversed the expanse of Yellowstone. The Sheepeaters, a band of the Shoshones, lived in its mountains. In 1807 the intrepid mountain man John Colter became the first documented white man to visit the region, after being excused from the return journey of the Lewis and Clark expedition. This took place as part of his amazing 500-mile solo journey through uncharted wilderness. Subsequently, other trappers from time to time would venture into the Yellowstone territory.

Jim Bridger and Osbourne Russell were two of the more renowned adventurers to visit Yellowstone, and even these two well-traveled gentlemen became caught up in its wonder and beauty. In 1835, while in what is now the Lamar Valley, Osbourne Russell recorded in his journal: "For my own part I almost wished I could spend the remainder of my days in a place like this where happiness and contentment seemed to reign in wild romantic splendor surrounded by majestic battlements which seemed to support the heavens and shut out all hostile intruders."[2] Jim Bridger, known for his tall tales, has been linked with many of the famous yarns about Yellowstone's natural features. He is credited with tales of petrified grass, petrified animals, fish

2. Osbourne Russell, *Journal of a Trapper*, Aubrey L. Haines, ed. (Lincoln: University of Nebraska Press, 1965), 27–28.

caught already cooked, and hunters aiming at elk only to find that their targets were merely reflections in glass mountains. While these stories were rightfully considered outlandish, they along with the more genuine reports caused people to listen and wonder about the facts concerning "the place where Hell bubbled up."

By 1840 the era of the trappers had ended and the region, for the most part, was once again left to the Indians. However, the 1860s brought the discovery and exploitation of mineral resources in Montana, and prospectors became interested in Yellowstone. In August and September 1863 an engineer named Walter DeLacy led a forty-two-man expedition to prospect the country that is now the park. The party explored the rivers, mountains, and geyser basins; but the only natural wonder they hoped to find was gold. Locating none, DeLacy did not feel it important to publish his journal, which he did not do until later. Concerning DeLacy's findings, historian Hiram Chittenden editorialized: "That he failed to publish his discoveries must be regarded as fortunate, so far as the park is concerned, for the time had not yet come when it was desirable that the real character of this country should be made known."[3] From 1863 to 1869 other prospectors inspected the region with similar results.

The combination of stories from trappers and miners about the land filled with curiosities motivated others to take a more serious look. In quick succession a number

3. Hiram M. Chittenden, *Yellowstone National Park* (Stanford: Stanford University Press, 1954), 54.

of explorations were made to discover and record "the real character of this country." The first, the Folsom-Cook-Peterson expedition, took place in 1869. It was followed in 1870 by the Washburn-Langford-Doane expedition, which spent more than forty days approaching and traveling through Yellowstone.[4] It is this "Yellowstone Expedition of 1870" that is usually credited with "discovering" (that is, making known) the area. Newspaper accounts, magazine articles, and speeches made by participants led to the Hayden Survey of 1871 (and subsequently of 1872 and of 1878).

The Hayden Survey was official. It was led by Dr. Ferdinand V. Hayden, a geologist who was granted an appropriation of $40,000 for the purpose by Congress. Well-staffed and equipped, it included a topographer, two botanists, a zoologist, an entomologist, a meteorologist, and a mineralogist. Maps were drawn, flora and fauna classified, geological features studied and noted, specimens taken, and place names conferred. Very important to this survey and the ensuing effort to create Yellowstone National Park was the inclusion of pioneer photographer William H. Jackson and landscape artist Thomas Moran, whose beautiful photographs and paintings of Yellowstone's wonders were shown to members of Congress. The efforts of this group and the resulting reports, articles, visuals, and speeches created an atmosphere of public and political concern for the

4. For an account of this expedition see Nathaniel Pitt Langford, *Diary of the Washburn Expedition to the Yellowstone and Firehole Rivers in the Year 1870* (St. Paul: J. E. Haynes, 1905).

preservation of the region.[5] On 1 March 1872 President Ulysses S. Grant signed the bill establishing Yellowstone as the first national park.

Once Yellowstone National Park was established, however, it was not long before officials realized that no one really knew what a "National Park" was, much less how to administer it. It took forty-four years of trial and error before a practical method of managing the park was created: the establishment of the National Park Service in 1916.

At first the park was run by a succession of superintendents appointed by the Secretary of the Interior. Their abilities and degrees of concern for the park varied from vigorous to haphazard. So also did their interpretations of what was meant by "administering." Another major handicap for these early managers was the lack of appropriated operational funds. Concern about the inefficient manner of administration reached a zenith in the early 1880s. This led to a decision to allow the United States Army to carry out the intent of the act that created Yellowstone Park. The army's stewardship began in 1886 and continued for thirty-two years; and the military did a good job. They brought order to the besieged park and and developed management policies, many of which are still in force. When the military handed the reins to the newly established Park Service,

5. For a discussion of the first Hayden survey see Richard A. Bartlett, *Nature's Yellowstone* (Albuquerque: University of New Mexico Press, 1974), 164–93. See also Ferdinand V. Hayden, *Preliminary Report of the U.S. Geological Survey of Montana and Portions of Adjacent Territories; being a Fifth Annual Report of Progress* (Washington,

Yellowstone was more secure and tightly organized than ever.[6]

In the ten years preceding Mary and Jesse Richards' visit, Yellowstone managers had had more than their share of problems and frustrations. Means of travel in the area were still rugged, but with each new year came more visitors, including VIP government officials, scientific explorers, wealth-seeking prospectors, sightseeing tourists, hunters poaching wildlife, and Indians futilely trying to maintain their lifestyle. Needless to say, their purposes and needs were often in conflict.

An incident in the summer of 1877 reminded all concerned that Yellowstone was still part of the lingering frontier: the war against Native Americans dragged through the park. About 800 Nez Perce from the Northwest were fleeing the prospect of life on a reservation in an attempt to reach the relative freedom and safety of Canada. Part of their zig-zag flight of 1500 miles took them through the middle of Yellowstone, where they ran into unsuspecting tourists and unfamiliar terrain.

With the military in pursuit, the Nez Perce forced an old prospector to act as a guide. Near Fountain Geyser, they abducted a group of tourists whom they later re-

D.C.: Government Printing Office, 1872); and F. V. Hayden, *Sixth Annual Report of the United States Geological Survey of the Territories . . . for the Year 1872.* (Washington D.C.: Government Printing Office, 1873).

6. For the U.S. Army's role in the National Parks see H. Duane Hampton, *How the U.S. Cavalry Saved Our National Parks* (Bloomington: Indiana University Press, 1971).

man managed to survive. In Hayden Valley, two
groups of visitors encountered the Nez Perce. One
party, headed by the colorful Earl of Dunraven (for
whom Dunraven Pass is named), escaped without incident. The other group was not so lucky: they lost one
member when they were ambushed while camping at
Otter Creek. Before they left the park, the Nez Perce
killed a second man from this touring party.

The leaders of the Nez Perce, particularly Looking
Glass, Poker Joe, and Chief Joseph, were very concerned about not harming civilians, since their fight was
with the military. Unfortunately, some of the younger
warriors were at times uncontrollable; this led to unnec-
essary confrontations and tragedies. After two weeks in
the park, the Nez Perce headed north through Montana.
Colonel Nelson Miles's forces caught them just forty
miles short of the Canadian border. Only after an intense battle did the Nez Perce surrender. It was there, on
the cold north slopes of Montana's Bear Paw Mountains, that Chief Joseph made his famous speech in
which he stated, "From where the sun now stands I will
fight no more forever."[7]

Hostile encounters with Native Americans were not
the only problems that early park superintendents faced.

7. See Joel C. Janetski, *Indians of Yellowstone Park* (Salt Lake City:
University of Utah Press, 1987). For a firsthand account of being
held hostage by the Nez Perce see Mrs. George Cowan's account,
which is reprinted in Paul Schullery, *Old Yellowstone Days* (Boulder:
Colorado Associated University Press, 1979), 1–25.

The vast size of the park enabled hunters to kill animals wantonly, a problem that persists in a lesser degree to this day. Squatters tried to occupy park land; visitors carelessly, sometimes purposely, caused forest fires; tourists threw a wide array of items into geysers and broke off chunks of geyser mineral formations. One example of vandalism, committed by the same people the Nez Perce had held hostage, occurred when they filled Old Faithful geyser full of stones, logs, stumps, and various rubbish in an attempt to see if they could jam it. However, Old Faithful successfully erupted on schedule and away flew "rocks, trees, and rubbish to a height seventy-five or eighty feet in the air."[8]

The profiteers descending upon Yellowstone posed a great threat to the very concept of a "national park." The railroad companies, particularly the Northern Pacific Railroad, and other economic opportunists were very keen on the idea of making Yellowstone a popular national summer vacation center. They did not want a natural, wild experience but rather something along the lines of such hot-spring resorts as Saratoga, New York, or Hot Springs, Arkansas. These entrepreneurs had very little interest in the preservation of Yellowstone; like the prospectors of twenty years before, they were in search of wealth. Their calculated goal was to draw more and more people to the park and thereby increase the demand for (and the profits from) stagecoach services, hotels, eateries, and bathhouses. While some of

8. Frank M. Carpenter, *Adventures in Geyserland* (Caldwell, Idaho: Caxton Printers, 1935), 64.

these services were established and were perhaps needed, it is most fortunate that Yellowstone was saved from the many efforts to make it a mere tourist destination rather than a sanctuary of America's wild natural heritage.[9]

Despite all of these problems, there were also successes. Some two hundred miles of road had been constructed by the time of the Richards' visit. However, these roads were built so quickly and through such rough terrain that many had stumps left in them, and other routes were very steeply pitched along the side of mountains. In addition to these roads, more than one hundred miles of bridle paths had been cut. But the most important success of all was that Yellowstone remained wild. Whatever the reasons, the remote location or the long winters without visitors, some credit must also be given to the efforts, no matter how seemingly inefficient, of the caretakers who loved Yellowstone and what it stood for.

In 1882 the geysers and mysteries of Yellowstone continued to catch the imagination of America and the world. Although the vast majority of people would

9. For a discussion of the efforts to monopolize and turn Yellowstone into a business enterprise see Aubrey Haines, *The Yellowstone Story: A History of Our First National Park*, two vols. (Boulder: Colorado Associated University Press, 1977) 1:261–91, 2:30–53; and Richard Bartlett, *Yellowstone: A Wilderness Besieged* (Tucson: The University of Arizona Press, 1985), 43–71, 113–67. See also Ellis P. Oberholtzer, *Jay Cooke: Financier of the Civil War*, two vols. (Philadelphia: George W. Jacobs and Co., 1907), 2:226–36. For an overview of the tourist businesses in Yellowstone see Chittenden, *Yellowstone National Park*, 110–13.

never set eyes upon the region, they craved information about this "National Park" and its "wonderful natural curiosities." During its first decade, only a total of 8,330 people visited Yellowstone.[10]

Writers became effervescent in their struggle to convey the feelings and visions they experienced in "Wonderland." Pioneer photographer Charles R. Savage introduced a newspaper article by stating: "Who has not heard of the Yellowstone Park, of its many marvels, of the weird and strange sights to be witnessed within its borders, of its glorious waterfalls, its many colored cañons, its mud springs, its spouting geysers, its sulphur mountains and wondrous lakes? Let those who have not heard bear with the writer in the effort to describe what he saw on making a visit for artistic purposes in this world-famed region."[11] Adjectives such as "awful," "grandest," "grotesque," "hell-like," "freakish," "devilish," "remarkable," "magnificent," "weird," "strange," "wondrous," and "beautiful" were common in these early efforts to describe Yellowstone to a populace that had to rely on the printed word. Due

10. Haines, *The Yellowstone Story*, 2:478. Haines estimates that there were 1,000 visitors to Yellowstone National Park in 1882. He based his pre-1890 estimates on these sources: 1) Letter, Governor Benjamin F. Potts (Montana) to Superintendent Nathaniel P. Langford, 27 November 1873, in the National Archives, Washington, D.C.; 2) Annual Report of Superintendent Philetus W. Norris for the year 1879, 22; 3) Annual Report of Superintendent Patrick H. Conger for the year 1882, 10; 4) Statement of Assistant Superintendent L. Henderson in Livingston (Montana) *Enterprise*, 16 July 1883, 1, 5.

11. Charles R. Savage, "A Strange Country, Geyserland," *Deseret Evening News* (Salt Lake City, Utah, 17 September 1884).

to the printing technology of the time, books and magazines had to use illustrations and engravings (sometimes based on photographs) for their visuals. These were often highly romanticized renderings which often embellished reality.

In addition to being animated, some writers would knowingly or unknowingly exaggerate what they saw. Without letting the facts get in the way, an author writing in the March 1882 issue of *Nineteenth Century* magazine bubbled with adjectives and slightly exaggerated in stating:

> Those who dwell in the vicinity of the Yellowstone National Park love enthusiastically to term it Wonderland. Nor is it altogether without reason. Within its boundaries (one hundred miles square) there are over 10,000 active geysers, hot springs, fumaroles, solfataras, salses, and boiling pools. Of these over 2,000 are confined in the small area comprising the upper and lower geyser basins. Sulphur mountains, an obsidian mountain, a mud volcano, and various other remarkable phenomena, add to the curiosity of this extraordinary region. Some of the grandest, some of the most grotesque scenery may be seen here, and the magnificent falls, the interesting cascades, and the eccentric beauty of the Grand Cañon may well challenge comparison with the world's most picturesque features. To attempt an exhaustive description of these marvels within the limits of letter-writing is impossible. Equally difficult is it,

amongst so much that merits attention, to select that
which is most noteworthy.[12]

Other sightseers rose above the mere use of adjectives. The artist Alfred Lambourne, for example,
"painted" this description of a waterfall in Yellowstone's Grand Canyon: "Amid all this glad acclaim,
hangs the great fall, most lovely of all. Even at this distance we can see the clearness of the water as it glides
over the lip of the fall, then it breaks into ripples of
creamy foam, like delicate lace around a lady's throat;
broader, deeper, they grow, forming festoons and
points of exquisite grace, through the interstices of
which pale emerald and opalescent blues reveal themselves; yet all moving swiftly downward to become
folds of billowy gauze, waving around the skirts of the
fall, and finally passing away in mist."[13] Lambourne
continued to portray Yellowstone in this same manner
through three and a half newspaper columns.

Yellowstone was also seen as a wildlife reserve, and
many appreciated the opportunity to view the extraor-
dinary variety of animals. As today, visitors took special
delight in seeing a bear, whether it was a "Griz" or a
black bear.

12. Francis Francis, "The Yellowstone Geysers," *Nineteenth Century* (March 1882): 369–77. The park is about 54 miles wide by 62
miles long, equalling 3,348 square miles or 2.2 million acres. It is
conservatively estimated that there are some 150 geysers and over
5,000 hot pools, hot streams, and steam vents.
13. Alfred Lambourne, "Impression Sketches of the Yellowstone," *Salt Lake Herald* (19 October 1884): 9.

A few visitors to the park, while impressed with the geysers and canyons, were really more interested in the fishing. The fishing got high marks, even if the fish sometimes did not. George Vest found "the fishing very good in the Yellowstone River," the trout plentiful in Black Tail Creek, and he thought the Snake River to be the "finest trout stream in my knowledge." However, he wrote that in Yellowstone Lake the trout were large and hungry, but "filled with parasites, and worthless for the table."[14]

It was in this atmosphere that Mary Richards wrote her very candid letters. Her letters take us back to Yellowstone National Park in 1882. She does not try to impress us with her writing style; rather, she speaks directly to us. Readers thus feel as though they are there with her. Her love of Yellowstone is evident throughout this volume. While at times she is effusive, she is, for the most part, much more subtle than many others who wrote about Yellowstone during this time. Like other authors, however, she seeks to have the reader "see" the things about which she is writing. For example, when describing a geyser field, she explains: "The eye cannot measure the depth of these cavities, but their incurved sides are like intricate carvings of translucent marble. All these pools have paroxysms of boiling and overflow. . . ."[15]

14. George G. Vest, "Notes of the Yellowstone Trip," *Field and Stream* (8 November 1883): 282.

15. Mary B. Richards, *Camping Out in the Yellowstone* (Salem: Newcomb and Gauss, 1910), 56.

Mary was well informed about the issues and changes facing Yellowstone. Her concern is stated when she discusses the future:

Tourists to "Wonderland" in near future seasons can and will dispense with camping outfit. They will "do" the tour in far less time in city clothes. The modern Hotel Fiend is now legally let loose by Uncle Sam in my arcadia. I know full well the followers in his train. Palatial cars will bear the traveler to the edge of the Park, where fences, toll houses, nurseries, malarias, regulations and high prices will begin. . . . The tent will be folded and laid away and the camp fire extinguished.[16]

She was right. Yellowstone was on the verge of change and would never be the same again. However, the park never got as bad as she feared. After 1882, Yellowstone would see ever-increasing numbers of visitors. The VIPs, the affluent, the middle class, and sometimes even the poor, each in their own style, came to fish and to see the wildlife, the canyon, and, of course, the geysers. In 1883 construction of the large Mammoth

16. Ibid., 54. Since she was from New York, one wonders if her fears were roused by the 16 January 1882 issue of the *New York Times*, which announced in a front-page article the plans of a group of wealthy men connected with the Northern Pacific Railroad company "to build a branch tourists' line from some point on the line, probably Bozeman, Montana, to the heart of the Yellowstone National Park, and erect there a large hotel for the accommodation of visitors. . . . The syndicate has exclusive hotel privileges for the park." The railroad branch line did not come to fruition.

Hot Springs Hotel was begun, and the hotel was in use by the summer of 1884. "Tent hotels" began to spring up throughout the park in 1883. By 1892, three considerable hotels were in operation: the Canyon Hotel, the Lake Hotel, and the Fountain Hotel. Some visitors, however, still continued to enjoy tents and campfires. Stagecoaches soon began to provide tours for visitors. Each year the road system was enlarged to meet growing demands.

When Mary and Jesse Richards made their trip, there were a good number of guide books and magazine articles available concerning traveling to and visiting Yellowstone. Since Mary seems well versed in the statistics, facts, tales, and history of the region, it seems likely that she had prepared for her trip by reading some of these.[17]

Her letters also present an intelligent, well-traveled woman whose good sense of humor allows her to have fun and to sometimes laugh at herself. In many ways

17. Some of the books that would have been available to her included James Richardson, *Wonders of the Yellowstone* (New York: Scribner, Armstrong, and Co., 1873); Edwin J. Stanley, *Rambles in Wonderland; or, Up the Yellowstone and Among the Geysers and Other Curiosities of the National Park* (New York: Appleton and Co., 1878); Robert E. Strahorn, *The Enchanted Land or An October Ramble Among the Geysers, Hot Springs, Lakes, Falls, And Cañons of Yellowstone National Park* (Omaha: New West Publishing, 1881); W. E. Strong, *A Trip to Yellowstone National Park in July, August and September, 1875* (Washington, D.C.: privately printed, 1876); and W. W. Wylie, *Yellowstone National Park, Or The Great American Wonderland* (Kansas City: Ramsey, Millett, and Hudson, 1882).

Articles about Yellowstone National Park could be found in magazines such as *Forest and Stream, The American Naturalist, Nineteenth Century, MacMillan's Magazine, American Field,* and *Harper's Weekly.*

these letters reveal as much about Mary Richards as they do about Yellowstone.

Who was Mary Bradshaw Ives Richards? Her Yellowstone excursion gives us a detailed slice of an otherwise elusive life. She was born in Salem, Massachusetts, on 4 February 1825. She was the eldest of five daughters and three sons born to William S. Ives and Lucy Gardner Ives.[18] Her father was a prosperous printer and owner of the *Salem Observer* newpaper.[19]

In 1839, at the age of fourteen, Mary was attending school in Charlestown (across the Charles River from Boston). In a rare surviving letter dated 2 July 1839 Mary told her mother that she had gone to a doctor to have a tooth extracted. The operation was somewhat unsuccessful as only part of the tooth was removed; Mary admitted that she cried a lot. In the letter, she commented on previous correspondence and scolded a sister for not writing. She expressed sorrow that she had lost her silver pencil and her silk handkerchief, and she included a list of piano sheet music she wanted sent to her. The postscript stated: "Love to everybody, take good care of the Piano."[20]

18. "Salem City Records of Births, Marriages, and Deaths; 1644–1867," vol. 2, 118, in Family History Library, Salt Lake City, Utah. All their children lived to maturity except for one son who died in infancy.

19. The *Salem Observer* was no longer owned by the Ives family when Mary wrote these letters. William Ives was a partner in the paper from 1822 to 1862. See C. Deirdre Phelps, "Printing, Publishing and Bookselling in Salem Massachusetts, 1825–1900," *Essex Institute Historical Collections*, vol. 124, no. 4 (October 1988): 289.

20. Letter from Mary Ives to Mrs. Ives, 2 July 1839, "William Ives Papers," Essex Institute, Salem, Massachusetts.

In 1850, according to the federal census, Mary was living with her parents in Salem. On 11 December 1855 she married Jesse Mayne Richards, who was originally from Norridgewock, Maine.[21] The 1855 *Salem Directory* indicated that Jesse Richards was a partner in two grocery stores in Salem, one of which was located next door to the home of Mary's parents. This most likely facilitated the couple's meeting and subsequent relationship. From 1856 on, Richards was no longer mentioned in the *Salem Directory*.

Jesse and Mary Richards probably moved to New York City, though there is no solid information about them from 1856 to 1876. However, Mary's father died on 12 December 1876, and in his will Mary and Jesse Richards were listed as living in New York City. Their residence was also recorded as New York City in her mother's will, which was written three and a half months before her mother's death in October 1882. Before, in between, and after these dates there is no mention of their names in any of the New York City directories or real estate records. This is curious, but the couple could have chosen not to be listed in a directory. As for real estate, they very well could have been renting their place of residence.

Mary and Jesse Richards spent some of this time traveling. In the first letter of this volume she stated that "the change in the appearance of the City of the Saints [Salt Lake City] since 1870 is great." She also mentioned

21. "Salem City Records," 118. Also, Harriet Ruth Cooke, *The Driver Family* (New York: privately printed, 1889), 353.

that she found the water of the Great Salt Lake buoyant, "more so than that of the Dead Sea; not bitter but much salter [sic]."[22] She made additional references throughout the book that indicate knowledge of, if not travel to, other places.

According to Mary Richards's nephew, John S. Driver, the Richards attempted to visit Yellowstone in 1877 (Driver says 1869; see note for explanation) only to be turned back by General Phil Sheridan's scouts because "Chief Joseph of the Nez Perce had gone on the War Path."[23] Also, in 1878 Mary privately published in book form a seventeen-page letter which she entitled *An Ascension on Mt. Blanc, Switzerland*.[24] This book is a discussion of the Richards' travels in Italy and Switzerland, as well as their adventures hiking on a glacier in the

22. Richards, *Camping Out in the Yellowstone*, 3 and 5.

23. This is stated in handwriting on the inside cover of the copy of *Camping Out in the Yellowstone* that is located in the Yellowstone National Park Library, at Mammoth Springs. The note reads: "Presented to Mr. A. C. Harwell by John S. Driver, nephew of Mrs. Richards who started from Ogden Utah with her husband and guides for the Yellowstone in 1869 and was recalled in few days by a scout sent out by General Phil Sheridan because Chief Joseph of the Nez Persez [sic] Indians had gone on the War Path." Then, in different handwriting: "Presented to Yellowstone Library, July 3, 1931 by C. A. Harwell."

The date of 1869 must be incorrect on two counts. First, it was in 1877, not 1869, that the Nez Perce were making their run through Yellowstone. Second, Yellowstone was not made a national park until 1872. The area was still rather primitive in 1869 and explorations were just beginning. It is highly unlikely that Mary Richards would have attempted a visit in 1869.

24. This book is based on two letters printed in the *Salem Observer* on 5 October and 9 November 1878. They were dated as having been written on 31 August from Bellagio, Italy, and 20 September from Pontressima, Switzerland.

Alps. Like her Yellowstone letters, this work shows an adventurous, expressive, and forward-thinking woman unconstrained by that period's expectations put upon her gender. For example, as she was hiking over a glacier, she and her party had to negotiate a crevasse. She stated, with her usual good humor, that "these blue chasms are more fascinating on canvas than when directly under your feet.... Now imagine Bloomer Number One forcing an unwilling foot into the track, taking a long breath and jumping so far beyond the opposite edge that a supreme confidence possesses her soul that she shall neither delay the train or be drawn ignominiously along by a rope."[25]

All this traveling indicates that the Richards were a couple who had sufficient money and free time to use in pursuits of their own choosing. During the later nineteenth century and early twentieth century people of means traveled. This was considered leisure time well spent in a quest for knowledge and self-improvement.

After their 1882 Yellowstone trip there is another gap of information about Mary Richards. The 1900 federal census listed her as a widow living once again in Salem. Two years later, her translation of the popular French book *Lives of Two Cats* was published.[26] She was 77 years old at the time. Mary lived in Salem from 1900

25. Mary B. Richards, "Climbing the Alps," *Salem Observer*, 5 October 1878. "Bloomer Number One" probably refers to her being a feminist or a woman unconstrained by social conventions. A bloomer is a type of women's undergarment invented in 1851 and named after feminist Amelia Bloomer.

26. Pierre Loti, *Lives of Two Cats*, M. B. Richards, translator, (Boston: Dana Estes and Company, 1902).

until 1905. The *Salem Directory* of 1906 stated that she had "removed to Chattanooga, TN." In 1910 the Salem publishing firm of Newcomb and Gauss published Mary's *Camping Out in the Yellowstone*. If she were still alive in 1910 she would have been 85. The date of her death is unknown.

Also unknown is the Richards' exact route from New York to Yellowstone. For those endeavoring to travel to the park in its first decade, there was a tedious, tiresome journey by stage and/or on horseback for several hundred miles. By the summer of 1882, the railroads brought the traveler closer, but travelers still had at least a long day's hard ride before they entered the park. From Chicago the tourist had the choice of two possible routes to reach Yellowstone. One option was via railroad to St. Paul, Minnesota, and then on to Billings, Montana. From there, travel was by stage to Bozeman or Livingston, where travelers could hire a guide and "outfit" to take them to the park. The other route was by way of the Union Pacific Railroad to Ogden, Utah, with a possible side visit to Salt Lake City. From either Salt Lake or Ogden the traveler could take the Utah and Northern Railroad to Beaver Canyon, Idaho. From Beaver Canyon, travel was by horseback, stage, or wagon to the west entrance of Yellowstone.[27] It is probably this latter route that Mary B. Richards and her husband took to Yellowstone National Park.

Today it takes a fraction of the time it took Mary and

27. To get to Yellowstone from the West, the tourist could ride the Union Pacific to Utah and then take the Utah and Northern to Beaver Canyon.

Jesse Richards to travel to Yellowstone National Park. Upon entering the park through one of five entrances, modern-day sightseers can rapidly travel along more than 350 miles of asphalt roads, leave their vehicles to stride along boardwalks to see the principal sights, and then move on to another. Whereas the Richards spent nine days in the park, modern visitors are unlikely to spend more than two or three days there. Today more than three million people anually visit the park versus one thousand visitors in 1882. For overnight lodging there are now cabins and hotels in six different locations throughout the park where tourists also can find such modern amenities as cafeterias, restaurants, grocery stores, curio stores, and gas stations. But one can also choose to use a tent or RV in one of several designated campsites. Gone are the days of camping wherever you find a spot. To come close to that experience one must obtain a free permit from the National Park Service to backpack the trails.

As one travels the roads and visits the various "spots," it becomes apparent that despite all the development there is still a great amount of open territory in Yellowstone. The majority of the park is still open and relatively untamed. The average tourist sees only from two to five percent of the whole of Yellowstone.

There are many modern problems pressing upon Yellowstone: grizzly-bear and other wild habitat is being lost to development and logging that push against the park's boundaries, a New Age religious enclave desires to tap into geothermal wells, a Canadian mining company plans to open a massive gold mine just two miles northeast of the park (yes, the prospectors are still searching for wealth), and oil and gas exploration con- tinues in the forests outside the park.

Yet in the face of all these (and more) threats, a visit to Yellowstone National Park is still a journey into beautiful and relatively wild nature. It is a place to see mountains, forests, meadows, moose, elk, coyotes, bison, bear (if you're lucky), and those "curious wonders"—geysers. Yellowstone is also a state of mind—one is transformed by the experience and never forgets the awe felt while there or by sharing the experiences transcribed by others—such as here by Mary Richards.

Enjoy this journey to the Yellowstone of 1882.

❧ NOTE TO READERS

The spelling and grammar of Mary Richards's letters are reprinted as originally produced, except in a few cases of obvious typographic error. Any changes that have been made have been done for the sake of clarity and are contained within brackets [ ].

William W. Slaughter

🍃 *Camping
Out in the
Yellowstone
1882*

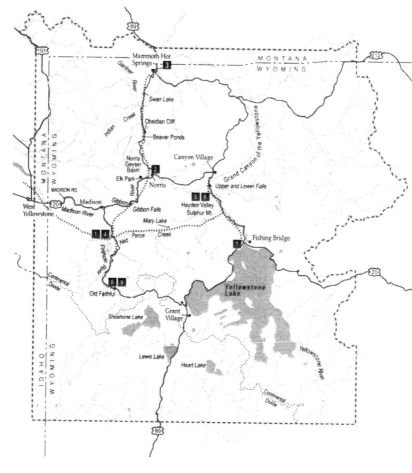

Camping Spots or Letters written

	Aug. 1,	1882	Camas Prairie
	Aug. 2,	1882	Lake Henry
1	Aug. 3,	1882	Fire Hole Basin
2	Aug. 4,	1882	North Fork of the Gibbon
3	Aug. 5,	1882	Mammoth Hot Springs
4	Aug. 7,	1882	Fire Hole Basin
5	Aug. 8,	1882	Banks of the Yellowstone River
6	Aug. 9,	1882	Yellowstone River
7	Aug. 10,	1882	Yellowstone Lake
8	Aug. 12,	1882	Upper Geyser Basin
9	Aug. 13,	1882	Upper Geyser Basin

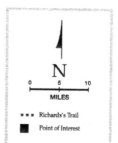

N

0   5   10
MILES

■ ■ ■ Richards's Trail

■   Point of Interest

❧ Salt Lake City

*Salt Lake City Revisited. A Service in the Mormon
Temple. Preparing for the Trip. The Equipment. First
Day's Journey and the Camp at Night.*

IN CAMP CAMAS PRAIRIE,
ROCKY MOUNTAINS,
AUGUST 1ST, 1882.

We are en route for the Yellowstone National
Park. On July 27th we arrived at Salt Lake
City where we purchased blankets and provisions. The
change in the appearance of the City of the Saints since
1870 is great. At the time of our first visit it was a peaceful place with neat houses, large gardens, and clear water running plentifully through its streets. Today we
find it full of busy, bustling people, many of them
Gentiles,[1] who rush thither amid street cars, saloons,
clouds of dust, a diminished supply of water, and war-

---

1. Gentile is a term used by Mormons for anyone who is not a
Latter-day Saint. Ironically, it also includes Jews.

4   contentions of business competition.

For many miles as we approached the city we noted a great increase in cultivated land. Thousands of acres have been irrigated by mountain streams forced into new channels by skilful and industrious Mormons. Labor and patience have conquered a desert of sand, salt, and sage brush; have banished coyote, owl and rattlesnake; and houses and barns of farmers stand in groves and orchards overlooking broad fields of grain and grass.

The Continental, formerly the Townsend, welcomed us to its cool piazza, broad portal and excellent table. The heat in sunshine, was intense and the dust aggravating. We made our purchases of blankets and provisions for camp outfit regardless of benefit conferred on Mormons, Jew or Gentile. Early in the morning of the 29th we visited the graves of Brigham Young and his first wife. An immense rectangular block of stone, worthy by its size of a place in Cheops, marks the "Prophet's" resting place; while "the wife's" beside his is unsodden and uncared for.[2]

---

2. Brigham Young, second president of the Church of Jesus Christ of Latter-day Saints (Mormons), was born in 1801 and died 29 August 1877. His body was buried in a private cemetery on First Avenue between State Street and A Street in Salt Lake City. Mary Ann Angel married Brigham Young in 1834, after the death of his first wife. Mary Ann was born in 1803 and died 27 June 1882, just a month before Mary Richards's visit, which may explain her grave's "unsodden and uncared for" condition. Cheops is the Greek name for the Egyptian king Khufu, who began his rule about 2650 B.C. and built the Great Pyramid of Gizeh.

Continental Hotel, Salt Lake City, Utah, ca. 1880. LDS Church Archives.

Black Rock and Garfield Landing on the Great Salt Lake, ca. 1882. Charles R. Savage. LDS Church Archives.

Afternoon found us deep in the waters of Great Salt Lake. Thither we went on a train of six open cars, loaded to repletion with warm and pleasure seeking denizens of the city. Portions of the lake shore have been named Black Rock and Garfield. At the latter point a long pier, doubly lined with bath houses stretches into the tideless expanse of blue. At the shore end is a modern restaurant of very modest pretensions where benches, beer, gingerbread and bathing suits may be had for nickels and dollars.

The lake is very large, its shores sinuous, and with the mountains so nearly encircling it, forms a picturesque background to the near and strangely grouped bathers and spectators. We found the water buoyant, more so than that of the Dead Sea; not bitter but much salt[i]er.[3] The bucket of fresh water placed in every dressing room is an absolute necessity for removing the salt which incrusts the skin on leaving the lake.

Sabbath morning the 30th, we joined the worshippers in the temple, a building whose egg-shaped roof figures in every picture of Salt Lake City.[4] The Temple is a strange and ugly edifice, constructed throughout in defiance of architectural grace, but answering the pur-

3. The salt content of the Great Salt Lake varies from approximately 14 percent to 27 percent. It changes inversely with the size of the lake, which varies year to year according to precipitation. The Dead Sea has a salt content of 24 percent of its volume. Ordinary sea water is slightly less than 4 percent salt.

4. In writing about "the temple," Richards is actually referring to the Salt Lake Tabernacle. Construction of the Tabernacle was begun in 1863, and the building was in use by October 1867. The Salt Lake Mormon Temple was completed and dedicated in 1893.

pose of its builders. Ten thousand persons can be simul-

taneously sheltered from sun or rain on comfortable seats; can enjoy perfect ventilation and hear distinctly the voice of a speaker or the faintest note of the organ. A choir of over a hundred voices took places: men on the left, women on the right of the organ. Between organist and audience was the pulpit, which comprised several rows of velvet-cushioned benches and many reading desks. Below these was a long table upon which were arranged vessels used in the communion service; viz., dozens of pitchers, baskets and two-handled goblets, all of silver or plated ware.

Among the apostles in the pulpit sat D. H. Wells, the successor of Brigham Young, but John Taylor was not present.[5] At each side of the choir and filling the entire width of the edifice were rows upon rows of Mormon elders, the majority of them gray-headed, serious-visaged men. We were given seats in the very midst of the Mormon multitude, below the pulpit and near the Lion fountain in the centre of the building. The splashing of four jets of falling water, the chirping of sparrows darting in and out over our heads, and intermittent squeak and babble of at least fifty babies in arms, gave a variety of sound before the singing of hymns began.

I studied the forms and faces of old and young men and women around me, and failed to discover aught

5. John Taylor (1808–87), in fact, succeeded Brigham Young as president of the Mormon church. Daniel H. Wells (1814–91) was a counselor to the Quorum of Twelve Apostles which, under the leadership of the church president and his counselors, is the governing body of the Church of Jesus Christ of Latter-day Saints.

*Central Salt Lake City, looking south, ca. 1881. Note the "egg-shaped"
Tabernacle and, to its left, the Temple under construction.
Charles R. Savage. LDS Church Archives.*

above or below commonplace in line or expression. A crowd of human beings in a civilized community is much the same. Doubtless here, as elsewhere, beneath calm, hard or passionless exterior are deep regrets, vain longings and many a breaking heart. After the singing of a hymn, ten elders took places standing side by side at the table below the pulpit, and commenced breaking large slices of bread in small pieces; these they piled up in baskets, on which blessing was asked by an apostle, and then distributed to the people, each basket being passed up one row of seats and down the next till empty. It was then refilled, blessed and passed as before.[6]

In a church of six or seven thousand communicants much time is required for this service and the text was announced and sermon commenced before the blessing of the water. No wine is used, and the preacher paused in his sermon while both bread and water were blessed. I thought of the miracle of the loaves and fishes as I saw bread and water appear in vast quantities, from I saw not where, on that long, narrow table. For over an hour the ten pair of hands were not idle, and excepting the baby movement and noise, the vast audience was still and reverent. But I must not linger at Salt Lake City.

We are here in camp. To me the life is new, and a daily record may be interesting to those who care to hear from a yet unexplored, unimproved pleasure ground. We left the city Sunday afternoon by the Utah

6. Richards is describing the Mormon ordinance of blessing and passing the Sacrament (Communion).

and Northern Railroad. At Ogden took a sleeping car for Beaver Canyon. All along this road are Mormon towns and villages where green fields, large barns, fat stock, and plenty of children are prominent objects. At Brigham, one of the largest towns, children brought cool milk, peaches, apricots and grapes to the cars for sale.

The scenery is wild and beautiful. After sunset the irregular ridge of mountains, at whose base the railroad runs, clothed itself in dark blue and purple shadows. Above and below its undulations the moon seemed to rise and set as we sped smoothly and rapidly northward. One after another the stars came out and our fellow passengers "turned in" till only ourselves remained awake to watch the wonderful beauty of the midnight sky.

At noon of the 31st we reached Beaver Canyon,[7] where our camp life commenced. The village consists of a dozen log houses, two saloons and a big water tank. Its citizens are bound to other parts of the world by railroad and a telegraph office. Here are located some half dozen of the Bassett Brothers, fine enterprising fellows of the true pioneer stamp, who undertake to prepare and carry you in and through the National Park in good form; to bring you out all right by the way you went in, or start you in line for the northern exit by way of Bozeman and the Northern Pacific.

A proposed journey to and a sojourn in the wilder-

7. Beaver Canyon, Idaho, is the present-day town of Spencer, which is approximately fifty miles north of Idaho Falls via Interstate 15.

ness, one hundred and ten miles distant from Beaver Canyon and sixty-five miles long by fifty-five miles wide, where dwell neither butcher, baker nor blacksmith, requires much forethought and preparation to make it a success. Selecting from our trunks the thickest and oldest clothing, a change of boots, a few towels, gloves and our rubber coats, we stowed them in an English hamper, scarcely larger than a champagne basket. This, with our blankets and a rubber sheet, fitted exactly under a seat of our wagon.

Our hotel at Beaver Canyon was a little log house, whose door opened almost into the village well. The water of this much-used well was clear and cool. We sent the big tin pail at the rope's end many times down for coolness and consolation during our days of hard thinking and labor. We slept under the logs one night, leaving at noon August first for the park, whose western boundary is one hundred miles distant from Beaver Canyon.

Our outfit (two persons), consisted of a wall tent, blankets, buffalo skins, axe, hatchet, nails, ropes, hammer and wheel grease; flour, sugar, lard, ham, eggs packed in oats, canned meats, fruits and jellies; a long tailed frying pan, bake kettle, coffee pot, tin plates, cups and spoons, knives and forks; a capital driver, an accomplished cook, two large balky horses and lastly the all important spring wagon, canvas-covered, large, strong, rather stiff in the joints, but possessing a fitness for its purpose which we soon learned to appreciate. This outfit cost us eighteen dollars per day.

Our driver, Ernest, is the son of a Mormon; he thinks he has about twenty-five brothers and sisters, children

Advertisement for the Bassett Brothers, the outfitting service Richards used. This ad appeared in the July 30, 1882, issue of the Salt Lake Daily Tribune.

of four wives. One of these wives is dead, another "put away," and the remaining two wives live with their husband. The entire family of children are adults and not one a polygamist, or polygamist's wife. Our cook, Peter, is a natural Bohemian. Born in Paris, he has lost his mother tongue in his wanderings in many lands. Loving nature and freedom, he has learned to earn his living wherever man, pushed by spirit of adventure, can exist. He has clear, honest blue eyes, a complexion like a Scandinavian, makes good bread, shoots a pine-hen on the wing, dresses, broils and serves it with a better than Delmonicoes sauce.[8] What more can we require of him?

❧ AUGUST 1ST—8 P.M.

WE ARE IN CAMP on Camas Meadows[9] twenty miles from human habitations. Our horses left home reluctantly;

8. "Delmonico's" was an elegant New York City restaurant known worldwide for its elegant service, imaginative menus, and excellent cooking.

9. Camas Meadows is the spot where the "Bannock Trail" begins. This was a Native American pathway that proceeded to Henrys Lake, over Targhee Pass to the Upper Madison Valley, up over the Gallatin Range near Mt. Holmes, and then down Indian Creek to the Gardner River; from that point, the path moved up to Mammoth Hot Springs, turning east and north across the northern sections of Yellowstone National Park. This trail ultimately went to the buffalo ranges of the Bighorn Basin. The Richards were basically following this route until they reached the area of the Madison River.

On 20 August 1877 Camas Meadows was the site of a fierce battle between a group of twenty-eight Nez Perce Indians and L Company of General Oliver Howard's command. The battle followed the Indians' attempt to steal horses from Howard's camp the day before. See Merrill D. Beal, *The Story of Man in Yellowstone* (Yellowstone National Park: The Yellowstone Library and Museum Association, 1960), 88–90.

one even laying down in harness to show his disap-
proval of the journey; a brief, forcible process of frontier
persuasion reversed his physical and mental position,
and we started for the Park at a speed that astonished
loungers by the village well. In a short time, however,
our four-footed friends settled calmly to their work and
Ernest assures me that henceforth no pet lambs will be
more docile. The distance from Beaver Canyon to
Lower Geyser Basin is about one hundred and ten miles.
We are to camp three nights on the route. This, our first
night in camp, is in a broad meadow from which the
Bassett Brothers have cut a crop of native grass. Part of
this has been drawn many miles away and part remains
stacked in an immense mass.

Our tent, white, taut drawn, stands near the margin
of a clear creek, across which we have seen several mink
swim. Inside our new home is our furniture, viz.: a bed
of blankets folded on a rubber sheet, our hamper for a
table, a wagon seat for a sofa, a candle set in a bottle for
an electric light, a tin wash basin, soap and towels on a
pile of grass for a toilet room—only these and nothing
more. On our western outlook rises a superb range of
mountains, their snowy tops still ruddy with sunlight
that has said good night to us. Northward other and
more distant heights still reflect daylight. All around us
is daylight and shadow.

One can follow the basic route of Mary Richards and visit the
marked battle site by traveling county road A2, which is a graded,
improved gravel road between Spencer (on I-15) and Henrys Lake
(on U.S. 20).

A camp fire, now having finished its blazing, is at work baking bread and boiling coffee and broiling pine-hen and ham. How hungry we are! The horses have drank deeply, are cool and contentedly munching their oats, of which we carry a large supply for their especial solace and reward. Our road today has been mostly level and will continue so till we reach the range that feeds the Great Snake river and its tributaries. We have forded many steep banked streams, and studied the working of the "brake" which, so well handled, holds the wagon in any position.

We have seen a small herd of antelope and scores of sage and pine-hens who run or flutter along directly in front of our horses as if inviting the sure shot of Peter's revolver. Here comes our welcome Granymede loaded with our late supper! The banquet hall is lit up, the collation spread on hamper and grass. Exit witnesses. Tent flaps lowered and tied. Leave us alone to our first supper and sleep so close to the bosom of mother earth.

🍃 The Journey Begun

*Coffee in Camp and Incidents on the Way. Horses
Urged on by Flies. Animals, Fish And Birds Enliven
the Scene. A Typical Plainsman.*

IN CAMP, LAKE HENRY,

NEAR TYGHEE PASS, ROCKY MTS.,

WEDNESDAY EVENING, AUGUST 2.

Another full day has gone. We are forty-five
miles farther on our way. Sounds of the axe
and a crackling fire awakened us before sunrise. We
looked out from our tent on a rosy sky, a lawn covered
with dew, and a misty range of mountains at whose
base lay the goal of our new day. Our boys had slept under the stars; their grey blankets still lay on the grass;
empty cylinders from which they drew themselves out
at dawn. Our horses, voluntarily returned to the wagon
from their night's free grazing, were patiently waiting
their breakfast. The stiff, cut stalks of grass inside our
tent were wet and cold. We aired our blankets by
spreading them on a frame of sticks, while we break-
fasted outside the canvas. Never was coffee so deli-

cious,—its aroma sweetened even that morning atmosphere! "Condensed Milk, Eagle Brand," a sigh shall lie down with every emptied can that goes to mark the trail of campers to Yellowstone National Park!

To strike a tent, clear table, feed and harness horses and to start was the happy occupation of an hour. We crossed a few low hills and entered the "Ten mile Meadow," whose sides are rolling and grassy as some of our western prairies. Here is a fine soil, gravel and rich loam, watered by never failing streams. Too distant markets and too severe winters are [the] only and perhaps insurmountable drawbacks to its settlement by agriculturalists and stock raisers. We forded the Snake River[10] twice, and on the road which is almost lost in boggy soil, high grass and reeds, the dreaded horse-fly made his aggravating debut. Later in the season he disappears, but this fact gave no relief to our animals. They needed no urging and quickened their pace. "Their load is nothing when a fly stings" said Ernest, and by and by we reached a high ridge beside the river where they were unharnessed for the noon rest, and a cool breeze banished their tormentors. The current of the stream was clear and we saw many large fish enjoying life in their way, while below us on a sandy point several white cranes slept, standing on one leg, totally oblivious of our vicinity. During the forenoon we saw two fine elk, and [a] large herd of antelope among which Peter wasted an ill-intentioned cartridge. Brant, wild geese and snipe were plenty, and we had a plump young pine-

10. Henry's Fork of the Snake River.

hen for supper, the savor of whose flesh surpassed that
of any November turkey.

Our afternoon progress was over level ground and
toward the still retreating mountains encircling Henry's
Lake.[11] It was past sunset when this gem of Rocky
Mountain Lakes, beloved and frequented by the red
man, coveted and conquered by the white, came in
view.—It is five miles long by two wide and lies at the
foot of mountains which nearly encircle it and rise
above it to a height of over three thousand feet. Forests
of pine, aspen and willow are reflected in its calm surface, which is five hundred feet below the summit of the
Tyghee Pass.[12] Many of the heights around are girdled or
banded with snow. The Lake teems with fish. Stories
told by fishers of their exploits with spear or hook and
line are too large for my pages. Wild game both four
footed and feathered abounds and waits only the appear-

11. Henrys Lake was named after the trapper Major Andrew
Henry, whose expedition came upon it in the summer of 1810. In
1922 the lake was enlarged by the building of a dam on the Henrys
Fork River.
    Robert Strahorn, a contemporary of Mary Richards, stated:
"Henry Lake and surroundings are well worthy a two or three days'
halt upon the part of those who delight in mountaineering, hunting,
fishing and sailing, or desire rest, and were such scenes grouped anywhere except at the gate of Wonderland they would be heralded far
and near as attractions worthy a jaunt across the continent." See Robert E. Strahorn, *Enchanted Land or An October Ramble Among the Geysers, Hot Springs, Lakes, Falls, and Canons of Yellowstone National Park*
(Omaha: New West Publishing, 1881), 6.
    12. "Tyghee" Pass is now named "Targhee" Pass. The pass was
named for a Bannock warrior/chief who was killed in 1871 or 1872
by Crow Indians. It was first spelled Tygee, then Ti-ge, and finally
Targhee. Its altitude is 7,075 feet.

ance of good hunters to surrender "life, liberty and the pursuit of happiness." A few rude cabins erected by Sawtelle, one of the first pioneers, stand deserted on the north bank, although fear of the Indians has passed away.[13] Our camp is close to a battle ground where the Nez-Perces were defeated. We are shown graves, marked by stakes, of soldiers who were killed during the fight.[14]

As darkness came on we reclined on the grass and were listening to a story about "a good Indian" when we spied far back on the prairie a horseman coming rapidly towards us. We were sixty-five miles from human habitations, we four alone, with only [the] courage of three men, one shot gun and a pair of revolvers for defence. I listened for a war-whoop, almost expecting to

13. After serving in the Civil War, Gilman Sawtell migrated west with his wife. They made brief stays in Iowa, where an infant son was born, and in Nevada before settling at Henrys Lake in 1868. Here Sawtell made a pioneering but futile attempt to raise cattle. He then turned his efforts to supplying trout to the miners fifty miles away in Virginia City, Montana. The Sawtells abandoned their ranch after the 1877 Nez Perce and 1878 Bannock wars made it difficult to conduct business. It was Sawtell who, in 1873, "extended his wagon road from Henrys Lake over Targhee Pass to the Madison River and up that stream to the Lower Geyser Basin in Yellowstone National Park." Later in these letters, Mary Richards's party will travel this route until it meets the Madison River, at which point they journey to the Lower Geyser Basin via the newly established route over the Madison Plateau. Sawtell Peak, which is five miles south of Henrys Lake, was named for this early pioneer. Aubrey L. Haines, *The Yellowstone Story: A History of Our First National Park*, two volumes (Boulder: Colorado Associated University Press, 1977), 1:80, 195; 2:443-44.

14. See the introduction for an account of the flight of the Nez Perce in 1877 through Yellowstone.

see a whole band of savages appear at the heels of the rider. Who, save an Indian, and a very bad one too, could ride like the coming guest! Before the laugh raised at my expense was over, a small Indian mare stopped as suddenly as if shot, by our dying fire. A man, once white, dressed in buckskin, leather fringed, and red flannel, shouted a greeting to our boys, calling them by name. He had seen the smoke of our fire and the cover of our wagon from the foothills where he had been looking at his traps, and had come down six or eight miles to [here] from Camas Meadow and the Beyond. He was a fair specimen of an Idaho frontiersman. Would that I could introduce him to you and to a civilization that he scorns. He was of fine form and feature; thin, agile, brown as a chestnut and with uncombed hair and beard. His eyes were clear and sharp, looking through instead of at you while he spoke. The past fifteen years of his life have been spent mostly in open air. It is said that a true frontiersman can rarely be persuaded to enter a house. His worldly effects were carried with him on the back of his mare. A rifle, belt full of cartridges, an awful looking knife at his side, a long-barrelled revolver stuck in the back of his pantaloons, a pipe tied into a string around his hat. When he goes far from a camp or his game traps he has a pack pony for blankets, cooking utensils, fishing materials, articles for preserving skins of larger game, and a small stock of clothing or groceries.

We are told that we shall meet many such men in the Park and its neighborhood. They catch and sell fish or game to amateur sportsmen, to chance travelling parties

Tent and wagon ("outfit") of the type used by Richards during her tour of Yellowstone. Camping in the Upper Geyser Basin, 1882. F. Jay Haynes. Montana Historical Society.

and occasionally during the season visit villages on the new railroad routes to sell elk, deer or antelope meat, thereby gaining money enough to carry them through the winter. During the season they hibernate, almost like bears in some den of a country saloon, where, when whiskey circulates, they wake up and tell "o'er true tales" of their summer exploits. For such men, horse, dog and gun take the place of home, wife and children, and I am glad to have seen and talked with a live specimen of the rare genus. He assured us that he made the road, over which we travelled from Beaver Canyon for the use of trappers and hunters, that the Indians never worried him, that game would follow the Indian, etc., all of which I try to believe. I must finish by candle light. Our guest has gone to sleep outside with his head on a saddle. He covered up the gun and pistol with my large plaid shawl. Heaven grant he may not consider it his game when he leaves before daylight!

❧ Making Rapid Progress

*Over a Hundred Miles on the Way. The Last Day's
Journey. Reaching the Park in The Evening. Prospector
Calls. Black Tail Deer for Supper.*

IN CAMP AT FIRE HOLE BASIN,

YELLOWSTONE PARK,

THURSDAY EVENING, AUGUST 4[3].

One hundred and ten miles since noon of August 1st. Our horses are large and strong;
they have chosen their own pace. We shall lie down tonight in the National Park, and near the first hotel built
within its boundaries.[15]

We broke camp early as will be our custom. We

---

15. The first hotel in Yellowstone National Park was a rough-
hewn, two-story log structure built by George Marshall. It operated
as the park terminus for the "Virginia City and Hot Springs" mail
and stage line. The site of this hotel is at the present-day picnic area at
the beginning of Fountain Flat Drive in the Lower Geyser Basin. For
a discussion of this building see Lee H. Whittlesey, "Marshall's Hotel
in the National Park." *Montana: The Magazine of Western History*
(Autumn, 1980): 43–51.

found the shawl folded smoothly; a half dozen superb salmon trout[16] left on the grass; our guest gone. Our appetites increase at each meal. Peter finds that he must shoot an elk or antelope soon, or failing in this, must be prepared to issue and share short rations of ham.

Tyghee Pass is a natural path through the first range that separated us from the Park. Its altitude is 7063 feet. The air grew perceptively cooler as we rode on, and flowers kin to many we found in Alpine regions grew in profusion. Beyond the pass extends a fine road for ten miles along the high bank of the Madison river. It is smooth and perfect as any macadamized[17] road in England. Our horses drank at every ford and we had leisure to gather a large bouquet of familiar flowers; Larkspur, Monkshood and Gentian, of unusually large size and depth of color. We have seen today antelope and deer feeding, an elk, badgers, and a large bear's track freshly made.

We lunched at Riverside,[18] a camping ground on the

16. Richards is most likely referring to the cutthroat trout (*Salmo clarki*), which is the most common native trout in this area. Its body color varies; the back can be steel gray to olive green with yellowish brown sides and a red-pink belly. It is spotted, with the spots becoming more closely grouped toward the tail. Its common name comes from the red markings on the underside of the lower jaw.

17. To macadamize is to construct or finish a road by compressing a layer of small broken stone into a solid mass, rounding the road for drainage, and stabilizing it with a binder such as concrete or asphalt.

18. Riverside was established as a mail station in 1880. It was also a spot where tourists traveling from Beaver Canyon, Idaho, or Virginia City, Montana, could layover for the night or, as in Mary Richards's case, stop for a picnic. It is about four miles inside the west entrance of the park.

shore of Madison river, here a broad, turbulent stream
bordered with great boulders and groves of tall pines.
Here a "Prospector," of the pure pioneer stamp made
his appearance leading a dusty, weary pack horse. The
man carried a pick, and a case which we afterwards
learned held instruments and chemicals for testing [the]
value of ores. Pointing to the river, the first words he
said were "Take a big drink before you start out! There
ain't a drop of water between here and Fire Hole Basin,
fifteen good miles!" A few qualifying words that he
used I omit for the "Observer's" sake. Unstrapping the
heavy load from his "compagnon du voyage" both hurried to the stream and plunged into its coolness. Learn-
ing from our boys that another party would follow in a
few days the "Prospector" put on the "Hunter"; examined his rifle and said he would camp there a day or two,
shoot an elk and a few antelope and give the meat to
whoever might choose to give him a little ham in ex-
change. We watched the child of fortune as whistling
cheerfully he set himself to preparing his dinner. His
horse, hobbled to prevent too distant straying, went
jumping up a side hill like a kangaroo and was soon
busy in the "bunch grass" which all horses seem to pre-
fer to more succulent herbage. The man, skilled by daily
practice, had a fire blazing in less than two minutes.
Taking from the pack the undonewithout frying pan
and tin pot he soon prepared a repast of antelope steak,
ham, hard tack[19] and coffee, which he ate and drank
from the utensils in which they were cooked,—and

19. Hardtack is a hard saltless biscuit made with flour and water.

with a relish and certainty of good digestion any one might envy. Then, sauntering to the nearest shade he stretched himself on the grass and seemed to sleep.

After an interesting and refreshing nooning, we saw that our animals received an extra amount of oats to cheer them for their coming climb, and started on foot ourselves for the summit, seven miles distant. The second range is by far the steepest, the new road leading directly across a bold spur of the Rocky Mountains.[20] Below this, on the other side lies the Lower Geyser, usually called Fire Hole Basin, at a height of 7250 feet above sea level. Divesting ourselves of all superfluous clothing we walked steadily upward, turning at every conquered height to breathe and to admire the panorama below. Our delighted eyes rested on verdant meadows, winding streams, undulating foot hills, green with dense forests of brown, black and white where fire and tempest had set their colors. Arrived at length at the summit after a three hours' walk we waited for our wagon, and enjoyed a new prospect.

20. The "new road" was established in 1880 by Yellowstone Park Superintendent Philetus Norris, who felt that the route along the Madison River to the Lower Geyser Basin was impractical because of its numerous river crossings. In 1881 Robert Strahorn stated: "At Riverside, . . . one road strikes directly across a bold spur of the Madison Range to Lower Firehole Basin, 12 miles away, and another, the old road, leads along Madison River through its upper cañon to the same destination, and consuming about the same distance. The mountain route now takes preference, because it does away with the necessity of fording the turbulent and sometimes dangerous river, and affords some exceptionally fine pieces of scenery." The route was part of the old Virginia City and Hot Springs line. It was also known as the Old Fountain Trail. Today it is overgrown and is not maintained as a hiking trail. (See Strahorn, The Enchanted Land, 7.)

The southern and western boundary of the Park, a grand semi-circular line of summits, many snow crowned, were in full view. The appearance of the wagon cover slowly rising over the brow of the hill was welcome. Our day was fast speeding. We were sad and glad to see the hind quarters of a fine black-tailed deer occupying our wagon seat. Peter had shot the unfortunate creature ten minutes after leaving Riverside.[21] Consequence, one less happy life in these glorious solitudes, four more varied suppers in our evening camp.

The descent to Fire Hole Basin, six or seven miles, was made in less than two hours through a thick pine forest. Not one drop of water did we see. We grew thirsty ourselves and inwardly excused one adverb and two adjectives used by our friend at Riverside. When the brake was applied, at the top of the last slide down hill, we took our first look at Geyserland. We saw at our feet a small story and a half hewn log house, the first hotel built in Yellowstone National Park. A few rough sheds and a tent adjacent formed the settlement, lying at the base of a steep cliff covered with tall pines. A brook of cold water coursed near the buildings. Between the hills we had descended, and the river running through the Basin, spread a wide velvety lawn where a few horses grazed. Beyond these were foot hills, with

21. In 1883 regulations were set forth to officially prohibit hunting within the park. "Previously, hunting had been allowed so far as was necessary to supply the wants of camping parties—a concession that practically operated as an unrestricted license." Hiram M. Chittenden, *Yellowstone National Park* (Stanford: Stanford University Press, 1954), 108.

groups and forests of pine and fir trees skirting a belt of white earth and sand, here and there broken in ridges or rising in regular cone shaped hillocks. Amidst the trees and from and above the white belt rose and floated columns, wreaths and puffs of steam, looking as if the white clouds of a summer sky had fallen, and were moving, lost and bewildered, in a strange region.

It is nearly nine p.m. We are thankful for the long weary day just past, thankful for its sights, sounds and its supper. We will waste no moment in discussing comparative merit of deer steak, potted chicken or fried ham, and find no opportunity for argument on the assertion that camp life insures dreamless and refreshing sleep.

❧ In Geyserland

Visit to Mammoth Springs. A Lake of Hot Water. The Canyon and Falls of the Gibbon. A Perilous Crossing. The Devil's Den. Gentian in Hot Water.

NORTH FORK OF GIBBON RIVER,
FRIDAY EVENING, AUGUST 4.[22]

The first sound that greeted our ears this morning was the music of meadow larks; the first sight, a tiny ground squirrel perched on the handle of a tin cup, busily nibbling a lump of sugar. He darted out under the canvas at our first movement. We are unaware of other matinal or nocturnal visits. Sub-rosa, I have endeavored every night to close all large crevices, left by inequalities of the ground between it and the tent

22. "August 4": In both the *Salem Observer* and the 1910 printing of *Camping Out in the Yellowstone* Mary Richards's 5 August letter appears before her 4 August letter. Here they are published in the correct chronological order.

edge, by judiciously placing therein handfuls of grass, brushwood, stones and spare tent pins.

Before leaving [for] the Mammoth Hot Springs this morning, we paid a hurried visit to the Geyser meadow, within view of our encampment. Crossing Fire Hole River by a foot bridge, we found a bath house of logs,[23] whose only tub was supplied with warm water flowing in from an open sluice-way laid from a boiling spring. The water flows from a symmetrical white cone ten or twelve feet below the river bed, is soft and pure, issuing at boiling heat from a great depth.

Walking a few rods over a hollow sounding calcareous deposit, we stopped beside a boiling pool, at least ten feet in diameter, close beside and separated only by a thin deposit of lime from the cold river, into which its steaming overflow fell. Within two hours time and a circuit of two miles we proceeded at first carefully, as footing seemed insecure, afterwards fearlessly over strange geyser soil, if such it may be called; it is neither wet, dry, hot nor cold, neither is it mud, stone, sand,

---

23. In the early years of Yellowstone National Park the waters of its hot springs were believed to be of therapeutic value for a wide range of ailments. J. C. McCartney had built a bathhouse at Mammoth Hot Springs by 1871. Other entrepreneurs soon followed his example at different locations in the park. In his 1883 guide to Yellowstone, Herman Haupt, Jr., stated that "bath-houses have been constructed, where a most delightful bath may be had, the hot mineral water acting on the system very happily, and leaving the bather in a splendid glow, with all his pores open and his skin clean and cool." Herman Haupt, Jr., *The Yellowstone National Park* (St. Paul: J. M. Stoddart, 1883), 45.

Bathhouses lost their popularity during the 1930s. They became unprofitable and were eventually discontinued.

lime, clay, magnesia, alum or brimstone, but a mixture
of all these and a thousand more ingredients.[24] It may be
of any thickness beneath your feet, from an eighth of an
inch to a thousand fathoms, and below is—who can an-
swer? Here we took our initiation step into the "Wonders of Geyserland."

We crossed shallow brooks of hot water, stood on the
thin verge of round, deep pools fathomless to eye or
line, watched their clear water seethe and boil, fall in
foamy cascades over their indented edges, or suddenly
becoming calm and smooth allowing us to approach
and see the varied color of the incurved sides of the basin
and the fringed or scalloped margins of their polished
rims. Most of these pools lie even with the surrounding
surface; some by incessant ebullition and deposit from
high cones more or less pyramidal and sufficiently hard
to bear the weight of a horse and rider. These cones and
pools regular and beautiful in shape alternate with what
we believe to be extinct or dried up craters, [and] cover
an area extending for many miles beyond the arid belt
before mentioned.

Guided by signs of white steam ascending before and
beside us, we found new wonders at every turn. Behind
a belt of sickly fir trees we stumbled upon a "Paint Pot,"
an oval orifice whose longest diameter must have been
twenty-five feet, filled almost to the brim with a mixture looking like liquid chalk. At one end this had a

24. The soil around the geysers and hot springs becomes impreg-
nated and hardened when the minerals from the thermal features are
deposited as geyserite or sinter.

bright pink color, at the other was white as snow. These colors blended imperceptibly and the whole mass was bubbling and boiling violently as if a great fire raged beneath its rocky cauldron. The ground all around was splashed and dotted with masses constantly ejected. A strange sound and perceptible tremor of the place where we stood, sent me quickly in a new direction. A slight boiling over of the "Paint" took place, then all was comparatively still again.

Not a hundred yards distant was a small innocent looking lake with a pine tree and reeds and grasses mirrored in its clear depths. Among the grasses I saw a profusion of the blue gentian. In gathering a cluster or clump, the roots came up easily and I found them quite warm. We approached and dipped our fingers to test the water, but quickly withdrew them, scalded and reddened for the day. On our return across a boggy meadow to our camp, we succeeded in believing that all the specimens, vegetable and mineral, which we had gathered, were of "no account," and that we had just begun to see the geysers.

The distance from Fire Hole Basin to the Mammoth Hot Springs is fifty miles of very bad roads. Stumps, set singly or in clumps at every hitable position, steep pitches both short and long, terminating invariably in either bog holes or a yard of corduroy, and perpendicular or soft bottomless approaches to the frequent fords make the way, like Jordan's "a hard road to travel."[25]

---

25. "Very bad roads" were the rule of the day. One writer traveling the same route stated that the "road becomes in many places sim-

Within the first sixteen miles we pass safely "Earthquake Cliffs" and Gibbon Falls and Canyon.[26]

The falls are one hundred and fifty feet high,[27] falling over broad boulders, which spread the large volume of water like a lace curtain, in its foamy breaking. He who would see this beauty from below must go to and return from the base of the cliff by an almost perpendicular path, unaided by hand rail or ladder. We forded the Gibbon twice. At the second crossing, a large tree had fallen lengthwise in the current, necessitating a detour in deep water and over obstinate boulders in the bed of

---

ply execrable, here running along the bank, undermined by hot springs, and there, out of despair, taking to the river-bed itself. The jolting was dreadful." Charles Whitmell, "The American Wonderland, The Yellowstone National Park," *Reports and Transactions of the Cardiff Naturalists Society* 17 (1885): 94.

These roads were built under the supervision of Park Superintendent Philetus Norris in the late 1870s. In 1878, with limited funds and a timely military concern due to the fear of an invasion from the Bannock Indians, a road was built that connected Mammoth Hot Springs with the Geyser basins. "It was hastily built (only thirty days of elapsed time for sixty miles of road) and crudely made. Grades were often so steep as to require double teams; stumps were cut just low enough to clear the axle of a Bane wagon; and bone-jolting corduroy was frequently used, but bridges seldom; sidehills were negotiated by laying logs parallel to the roadway on the low side and scraping down a little earth and rock against them." (Haines, *The Yellowstone Story*, 1:242.)

It is approximately forty-five miles on the present road from the Lower Geyser Basin ("Fire Hole") to Mammoth Hot Springs (and fifty-one miles from Old Faithful in the Upper Geyser Basin).

26. The Richards party is traveling the road built by Norris in 1878, a portion of which proceeds along the foot of this rhyolite cliff. "Earthquake Cliffs" got its name because of frequent rockslides which appeared to have been caused by earthquakes. These cliffs are on the south side of the Gibbon River.

27. Gibbon Falls is eighty-four feet high.

Fording the Gibbon River, 1884.
F. Jay Haynes. Montana Historical Society.

the stream. A triumphant exit, however, proved the strength of both horses and wagon; our goods getting some wet from water reaching them to the depth of several inches.

The road continued rough through the canyon, leading close to the river and at the base of cliffs rising many thousand feet above us. The scant soil clinging to their steep sides seemed only held in place by bare trunks of a myriad of fallen pine trees, which lay piled upon each other at every possible angle. At one point the cliffs rise from the river too steeply to allow building a road, and we passed along some distance in the bed of the stream.

Soon after our entrance to the Canyon of the Gibbon we stopped in mute astonishment before one of the most awful spectacles of the Park. At the top of a great half cone of solid stone projecting into the river below, from the walls of the canyon, is the "Devil's Den," "Blower," "Roarer," or it can be called any other pet name.[28] From a horizontal orifice five or six feet wide and equally high, a torrent of boiling water completely filling the space poured in a basin directly below, whose depth all soundings have failed to determine. This cavity is forever full and overflowing. Frightful sounds, explosions of pent up water and steam, hissings, roarings,

28. Robert Strahorn's 1881 account of traveling in Yellowstone mentions, but gives no name to, this formation: "Soon after entering this defile [Gibbon Canyon] we heard a puffing sound like the steady pulsations of some monstrous engine. A short curve in the road soon revealed the secret. An aperture in the perpendicular wall on our left, some five feet in diameter, was sending forth a volley of steam with a boom-boom-boom that never ceases, but beats as regularly as tick of a clock." (Strahorn, *The Enchanted Land*, 17.)

and earth shaking generally, made conversation or re-mark inaudible. In fact, one finds very little to say in presence of such a monstrous exhibition. Every blade of grass and leaf trembled as if in terror. Our horses seemed entirely at ease, stepping aside a little to avoid the overflow of hot water, which ran beneath their hoofs and down the steep slope to the river. All through the canyon are hot springs flowing or spouting, color-ing the banks with varied sediments or whitening for a few rods the clear flow of the Gibbon.

Emerging in an hour from this deep and wonderful valley, we came into Elk Park, a charmingly smooth and peaceful looking camp ground.[29] The river winds to the left, and a group of fine pines stand close to a guard of high piled boulders on the right of the entrance. Blackened logs, tin cans, and bits of pasteboard, or pa-per lying about, told the tale of former and recent campers.[30] Our horses, being still fresh and ambitious,

29. Elk Park was a very popular camping ground in the early days of the park. It is approximately a mile south of Norris Geyser Basin.

30. Littering, along with vandalizing of geysers, was a constant problem of that period. In 1884 assistant superintendent James H. Dean lamented the fact that "each morning I look over the Geyser Basin, observe the action of tourists, remove all debris that may be thrown in the geysers, springs, pool, etc. I then proceed to Gibbon Meadows . . . giving my attention to campfires that may have been left burning. I always have a shovel with me for this purpose, . . ." (James H. Dean, Report, 14 August 1884, Doc. 1356, Yellowstone National Park Archives.)

Herman Haupt chastised the vandals, maintaining that "every intelligent visitor should feel sufficient interest in this museum of na-ture to frown upon the barbarism of persons who come with axes and hammers to break up and carry away baskets full of the coral-like formation around these craters." (Haupt, *The Yellowstone National Park*, 89–90.)

"Gibbon Boiling Springs," Beryl Spring, Gibbon Canyon, 1884.
F. Jay Haynes. Montana Historical Society.

we decided to go forward six miles before camping, promising ourselves to stop on that spot and visit the "Monument Geyser," and "Devils Paint Pots," near by, on our return to Fire Hole Basin.[31] A ford over a hot water stream, "Geyser Brook," was made, and a range of hills crossed, some of them green, some destitute of vegetation, and some covered with the indescribable calcareous and sulphurous deposit, and many little meadows, uneven and spongy with extinct craters and their half hardened overflow of lime and mud.

Our road then led over a geyser basin, supposed to be the oldest in the Park, and once the scene of immense activity, whose area comprises twenty-five square miles. Prominent among the still living and working geysers are the "Monarch" and the "Minute Man," the latter a spouting geyser that ejects a forty foot column of water every sixty seconds, day and night. Between these regular performances the water sinks back in its bowl, and we could see some distance down the narrowing sides of white and yellow stone.[32]

31. Richards is referring to Monument Geyser Basin at the north "entrance" of Gibbon Canyon, just south of Gibbon Meadow. Apparently she and her group had planned to explore this area if they had camped in "Elk Park."

32. This is the Norris Geyser Basin. The road now travels around this basin; however, the "original" road went through the basin, passing near the present museum.

In his tourist manual, Henry Winser writes that Norris Geyser Basin "is apt to astonish and bewilder the neophyte in Wonderland, by its spouting geysers, clouds of vapor and overpowering odors of sulphur. . . . The whole vast basin is a collection of hot springs and pools varying greatly in color, some being jet black, some white as driven snow on mountain height, and other as sulphurous a yellow as Lucifer could desire. There are numerous fumaroles and solfatari, be-

The Norris Geyser Basin, 1881.
F. Jay Haynes. Montana Historical Society.

The Monarch has washed away a great circle of soil and rock all around it[s] premises; there were no signs of any very recent eruptions and deep crooked cavities that led down, down, down, nobody knows where, were dry and quiet; steam, however, ascended to the sky all about them. In fact, the whole surface of hill and meadow seems almost ready to burst with pent up heat and steam. Several times on attempting to gather crystals of alum or sulphur, I was smartly burned by the invisible heat, and twice, on dipping a cup into a spring, I found the water more than luke warm.

One fact still fills me with wonder. The blue gentian loves hot water. No other flower grows in such profusion where warm streams flow from these mineral sources. I have gathered it to-day near both wet and dry surfaces, where my feet, protected by heavy soles, found uncomfortably hot footing. The first vegetation that ventures to try life on a cooling geyser surface, is a sort of evergreen we call "Snake Bed." It is followed by diminutive seedlings of the purple aster, and a baby sunflower, then a course grass, all seeds and little blade, creeps nearer the still steaming cavity, and then, up comes the delicate gentian, small, blue, and fringed daintily as ever. Who could have suspected such a choice of a residence by that blue-blooded blossom![33]

---

sides 'frying-pans' which sputter and sizzle violently. The earth rumbles and shakes, and the air is hot and reeks with unpleasant odors." Henry J. Winser, *The Yellowstone National Park; A Manual for Tourists* (New York: G. P. Putnam's Sons, 1883), 28.

33. The "blue gentian" is the fringed gentian (*Gentiana thermalis*). It has deep blue petals with delicately fringed edges.

As we rode over that great basin we saw its grey and white surface dotted with pools of every color, most of them lying in round rimmed receptacles varying in width and depth, but all overflowing and mingling their waters in a stream flowing fast to the valley.

It was late when we gladly halted here and prepared our weary horses and ourselves for the night's repose. A long corduroy bridge, the champion of its kind for unevenness, varies the outlook on tomorrow's road. Just before sunset we met Jack Baronett on his way to Elk Park, where he means to camp to-night. He is a noted pioneer and scout, and built the first bridge over the Yellowstone River. He has two fine looking horses, and would have told us stories by the camp fire had we stopped at his chosen place to-night. [34]

34. It is unfortunate that Mary Richards did not hear Jack Baronett's stories, for he had some grand tales to tell. Her statements about Baronett (1829–1901) are correct, but there is much more to this man.

During his 1875 trip to Yellowstone, General William E. Strong described Baronett as "a celebrated character in this country, and although famous as an Indian fighter and hunter, he is still more celebrated as a guide. His knowledge of the mountains, rivers, and trails of the Western Territories is very extensive, as he has traveled over the greater part of California. From early boyhood he has lived in the mountains, and his whole life is a chapter replete with adventure and hair-breadth escapes. When Mr. Everts was lost on Doane's expedition, in 1870, and wandered for thirty-seven days among the mountains and cañons of the Yellowstone, living on roots, wild berries, and grasshoppers, Jack Baronette found him, on the fifteenth day, brought him in, and saved his life. He is highly esteemed by those who know him, and his word is as good as gold. He is of medium stature, broad shouldered, very straight, and built like Longfellow's ship, for 'strength and speed'; eyes black as a panther's and as keen and sharp; complexion quite dark, with hair and whiskers almost black. He speaks well, using good English, and his manner is mild,

In selecting a site for outdoor life, noon or night, wood and water are first essentials. We were warned by a croaker that we should find nothing but hot alum water for our bath, our horses and our coffee to-night. Ernest, who knows something of this wilderness, replied that the North Fork "ran cold water unless it had changed within two years." To our great joy it still runs cold water.

---

gentle, and modest, is proud of his knowledge of the mountains and of his skill with the rifle." General W. E. Strong, *A Trip to the Yellowstone National Park in July, August, and September, 1875* (Norman: University of Oklahoma Press, 1968), 47–48.

❧ Tramping and Camping

Two Runaway Horses. The Glass Mountain. Swan Lake, Terrace Pass and Willow Park. The Geysers.

MAMMOTH HOT SPRINGS,
SATURDAY, AUGUST 5, 1882.

While we and our horses were breakfasting this morning, two horses came galloping toward us from the direction of Elk Park. A man followed, shouting to Ernest to stop them at the bridge. We recognized Jack Baronett, whose horses had left business and started back for Montana, their birthplace, some hundred miles distant. Ernest and Peter each seized a halter, and each led and held a horse across a narrow bridge, thus effectually blocking the retreat of the faithful steeds. When their owner reached them they commenced rubbing their noses against his breast and arm, as if to say, "this behavior is all a joke, we are delighted that you ran all these miles after us." The trio

Obsidian Cliff with Beaver Lake in the foreground, 1884.
F. Jay Haynes. Montana Historical Society.

were soon returning to Elk Park to camp, saddle and pack. We foresee that the "hobbles" will grace two pair of slender forelegs to-night.

Our road to-day has been one of thorns, but the unique scenery has made amends. At Beaver Lake among its willows and tall rushes,[35] we met a pack train of ten mules, four horsemen and a large dog, "bound from the northern forts with supplies for a government surveying party which they expect to meet in the Park."[36]

Rising from the lake is a great curiosity, worth a thousand mile journey to see. A mountain, with outlying palisades and columns of obsidian, or volcanic glass.[37] It is a black, brown or a reddish yellow, is ex-

35. Early visitors to the park delighted in and made mention of this body of water. In his guidebook, Henry Winser informs the reader that "this lake was formed by beavers, who have obstructed the creek and constructed a series of thirty or forty dams, which sweep in graceful curves from side to side, each having a fall of from two to six feet in a distance of two miles." (Winser, *The Yellowstone National Park*, 27.)

36. During the summer of 1882 there was a considerable amount of road improvement and surveying taking place throughout the park.

37. The "columns of obsidian" is the Obsidian Cliff. Mary Richards's description of how a road was built over the obsidian is accurate.

Mountain man Jim Bridger was one of the first to note the existence of this natural feature in what would become Yellowstone National Park. One of the several Yellowstone tales attributed to Bridger includes this outlandish story about the Obsidian Cliff: "Oncet I camp yonder in a purty meadow. Wantin' meat I went lookin' fer an elk. I seen a beaut a right smart spell yonder. Comin' close, I let him have it. Bejabers, he didn't make a move. I moved nigh onto him—took a dead bead. Same result. Say I, I'll get so darn nigh the report o' the gun'll kill him. So I did. The blame critter

tremely hard and was used by the Indians for arrow heads, weapons and tools. The only method of making a wagon road or even a foot trail over its smooth sloping sides, was to subject it to alternate heating and sudden cooling by fire and water. This caused huge cracks and splintering of the surface, and by pick and axe vigorously applied, a rough, narrow road of broken glass is made; probably the first and last of its kind on our continent. A photographer and his assistant were there, looking as if they had felt "nature in her wildest mood." They were trying to find a good position from which to take pictures of this strange mountain and its surroundings.

Willow Park, Indian Creek and Swan Lake were passed in the early afternoon.[38] At Indian Creek we found groups of trees, whose bark had been recently peeled by squaws for cooking, and three fine tepee poles

---

didn't look up. O' course, I thought he was deaf, dumb, and blind. I was so bloomin' mad I grab my blunderbuss by the shank an' start runnin' direct fur him, intendin' to smash him slam-bang on the haid. Well siree, ye'd never believe it! What I act'lly hit was the side of a glass mountain . . . crawlin' to the top, what do I see but that same elk way yonder, feedin' as peaceable as ye please." (Beal, *The Story of Man In Yellowstone*, 113.) See also Chittenden, *The Yellowstone National Park*, 41–45.

38. Willow Park, Indian Creek, and Swan Lake are all so named today. Willow Park, about two miles north of the Obsidian Cliffs, is an open valley that was especially favored for camping by tourists entering the park via Mammoth Hot Springs. Indian Creek, a tributary of the Gardner River, was so named because of the Great Bannock Trail which runs along its north side. Swan Lake was named for the numerous trumpeter swans seen on this lake and in the ponds of the area.

left behind among some bushes. Peter tells me that the ground end of these tall slender poles so sharp and smooth, is made so by dragging for miles behind a pony.

Swan Lake did not belie its name. We saw many water fowl in its vicinity, tame and undisturbed by our presence, and near a shelving bank, floating slowly on the unrippled surface, a little fleet of snow white swan. Beautiful denizens of the woods and waters! May it be long ere the merciless shot of a civilized intruder disturbs your peace!

After a short but disturbed struggle with a range of hills, we entered the Terrace Pass[39] that separates us from a view in the gorge in which the Hot Springs are situated. We learned that the descent, a distance of three miles, was extremely steep and difficult for our horses. The ascent would be still more so. We decided to walk down, leaving our wagon for the night by the roadside. The boys were to pack a few necessities of food and shelter from the night air, on the backs of the horses and lead them down to eat their oat supper and breakfast below. "Property like a heavy wagon is safer anywhere than a pair of good horses" said Peter, "and we shall want them for company." So we lowered and fastened the side canvas and left the wagon and its contents, moored in a bed of ripe, wild strawberries, close to the road.

We soon came to openings in the trees through which we had glimpses of a wonderful gorge, deeply sunken

39. "Terrace Pass" is Terrace Mountain.

Pulpit Terrace at Mammoth Hot Springs, n.d. T.J. White. LDS Church Archives.

fifteen hundred feet below the pass. Hills, plains, terraces and bare white or yellow slopes came in view. Not until we reached the "Devil's Thumb" and stood by the gate of the enclosure surrounding the residence of the superintendent of the Park,[40] whereon is inscribed "No animals permitted to enter this gate," did we take in the strangeness of the scene.

The main terrace from which the hottest and largest springs flow is over a thousand feet above Gardiner River. Below this ridge, composed of great basins from twenty to forty feet in diameter, are hundreds of other terraces and basins large and small, into which the water boiling from the upper reservoir falls in its never ceasing overflow. Some of the basins are round, others oval or semi-circular and all are attached to the main formation, which is a vast pyramid resting on a base of a white and reddish line. Each basin, however small, has its beautifully wrought rim, its own peculiar form and color of lining. All are full and overflowing, bathed from summit to base in the mineral charged water. The colors displayed are not to be described. One can walk easily and securely from basin to basin on their hard margins, so constantly renewed or increased by sediment of the flow

40. The superintendent at this time was Patrick Conger (1819–1903), who had been appointed 1 April 1882, replacing Philetus W. Norris. He was the third superintendent of the park. Yellowstone historian Hiram Chittenden said of Conger: "His administration was weak and inefficient and brought the park to the lowest ebb of its fortunes. Its only palliating feature, as viewed from this distance, is the fact that its very weakness aroused public sentiment and paved the way to reform." His term ended 9 September 1884. (Chittenden, *The Yellowstone National Park*, 106.)

The Norris blockhouse on Capitol Hill at Mammoth Hot Springs, the super-intendent's residence to which Mary Richards refers.
Yellowstone National Park Archives.

from the upper and great springs. Part of the overflow reaches the Gardiner River,[41] part disappears in caves and crevices that abound in its vicinity.

Facing the terraces, and on the very summit of a small hill opposite, is the private residence of the superintendent of the Park. Water used for house-hold purposes is carried thither in barrels from a brook flowing a quarter of a mile below. By this brook, whose clear, cool water renders this place inhabitable, is the "Hotel", a small log house of three rooms; the second built in the Park. The owner, J. C. McCartney,[42] vacates his abode for the season and dwells outside. We saw him early this morning followed closely by a dog and a cat, who share with a favorite horse, his protection and care.

As recently as 1877, Indians drove away the half-dozen residents and visitors to this place, shooting fatally the owner of a log shed as he stood in his own doorway. His body lies on the other side of the brook, and is marked by a rough wooden bath tub in which he was placed for burial. Finding the improvised coffin too large, and the grave too small, they took out the corpse and placed it uncovered in the ground.[43] The bath tub [is]

41. Gardiner River is the same as Gardner River. Until 1959 the "i" in the spelling of Gardner was inconsistently dropped or added. "Gardner" is now the standard spelling.

42. "McCartney's hotel" was James C. McCartney's home, which he built in 1871, a year before Yellowstone became a national park. It would later be used as a laundry until it was destroyed by fire in 1913.

43. Richards is referring to Richard Dietrich, a music teacher from Helena, Montana, who had the misfortune of visiting Yellowstone at the same time the Nez Perce were pushing their way through the park in an effort to escape U.S. troops. Dietrich did not own the

J. C. McCartney's "hotel," Mammoth Hot Springs, 1882. It was on the doorsteps of this cabin that Richard Dietrich was killed by a group of Nez Perce in 1877. F. Jay Haynes. Montana Historical Society.

waiting removal. It may be used in some coming season, when lures of "healing streams" and "Bethesda Pools" draw scores of invalids hither hoping for relief or cure.

The tout ensemble of the entire scene from the piazza of the superintendent's house is unique. These peerless springs, whose still bubbling pools bear colors the eye vainly seeks in sky or on earth; whose basin walls of graceful form and glowing hues were unsurpassed in palace baths, dreamed of or built by Akbar for his houris;[44] set as it were in a frame of outlying forest, hill and mountain, form a sublime picture which waits the hope and despair of the coming artist.

"log shed"; he was part of a group of ten tourists from Helena who, while camping at Otter Creek near the falls of the Yellowstone River, were attacked by a group of Nez Perce. One of the party was killed; the rest escaped. Two escaped to the Madison River and out of the park, while Dietrich and the others went to Mammoth Hot Springs.

Most of the party left the park, but Dietrich and a couple of his companions stayed. At this same time, a band of Nez Perce, who remained behind the main body of Indians, ranged widely from the Yellowstone River to the Gardner River and up two miles north of the park, where they burned and looted a ranch. As they returned through Mammoth to rejoin their people, they surprised Dietrich and shot him as he stood on the steps of J. C. McCartney's cabin. While this was happening, one of Dietrich's friends, with the help of McCartney, was returning to Otter Creek to retrieve the body of their slain comrade. His other friend took off when he noticed the Nez Perce coming into Mammoth. Dietrich's body was found, still warm, by federal troops. His friends buried him nearby and then returned six weeks later and took his remains to Helena for reburial.

See Joel C. Janetski, *Indians of Yellowstone Park* (Salt Lake City: University of Utah Press, 1987), 73; Chittenden, *Yellowstone National Park*, 134–39; Haines, *The Yellowstone Story*, 1:233–37.

44. An houri is an alluringly beautiful young woman. Also, in Mohammedan belief, an houri is one of the attractive maidens with whom the blessed will live in paradise.

We extended our ramble below the brook of cool water, which, after supplying the settlement and a pasture actually sinks into the strange soil, leaving no sign of its previous and useful existence.

Beyond the foot of the gorge we saw the road to Bozeman, like a thread winding about the barren hills. We found a wide meadow, an unmistakable ancient geyser ground, clothed with a sparse vegetation approaching as if with careful steps to the verge of extinct "Spouters and Roarers." We came often to great circular cisterns abruptly sunken in a depth of from ten to a hundred feet from the level. In the bottom of one of these lay the bones of a large animal. We also saw many cast off skins of snakes. This meadow offers very few inducements to settlers or campers.

We were told of a traveler who, awakened in the night by a noise [he] supposed to be thunder, found himself, his tent, his horse and other belongings, all unharmed at the bottom of a deep pit. Of course he was resurrected, else whence the story? Peter's short speech as he gazed down one of the biggest the deepest holes tells volumes, "There's no dump to these pits; a piece of the world fell in, that's all."

A rough ladder made by thrusting long pegs of pine through the trunk of a tree, assisted us to descend and explore a narrow cave, whose entrance is at the bottom of a shallow depression. It was getting dark and the walls of the cave sloped so irregularly that little light entered. We found a hard footing, but could not advance far as we had neither guide, candles or on my part incli-

nation to linger in this very throat of a once great spouting geyser.

We returned somewhat tired to camp. The boys,
busy getting supper, reported the horses' dislike of the
air, water and grass of the Mammoth Hot Spring gorge.
We voted unanimously, being in Wyoming my voice
counted,[45] to leave early tomorrow morning for our
wagon; to breakfast there and endeavor to camp in the
afternoon in Elk Park.

---

45. The Wyoming Territory gave women the vote in 1869; the
first state/territorial government to do so.

❧ Wonders of the Park

*The Return from the Hot Springs. The Monument
Geysers and the Tigers. Brilliant Colors of the Devil's
Paint Pots. A Government Surveying Party
Encountered.*

FIRE HOLE BASIN,
MONDAY EVENING, AUG. 7.

We reset our tent to-night on the same rec-
tangle of grass where we slept the night of
August 3rd, having returned from a most interesting
trip to the Hot Springs, a distance of one hundred miles.
We left camp at daylight, August 5th, after a night of
heavy rain, and ascended the brims of the great pools for
a farewell look. All were enveloped in clouds of steam,
dense and rosy in the morning air. Walking slowly up
the steep and lonely road, unmarked by wheel or foot-
step we remarked the all pervading silence, the dewy
freshness of leaf and flower, and remembered that it
was good to be alive and well in the perfect Sabbath
morning.

A mile below the Pass we discovered a lake[46] lying a few rods to the left of the road. It was almost concealed by tall pine trees, whose boughs sprung from their trunks to the earth. The water of the lake was clear, boiling gaily from its center. Testing its heat with our hands we found it exactly right for a bath, which we proceeded to enjoy; R. swimming circuitously to the opposite shore, reporting the water clear, but near the center as too hot for comfort. There were plenty of toilet rooms, built years ago, secluded, convenient, and beautiful. An astonished bird on the boughs above, made musical observations on our appearance.

Our wagon and contents were undisturbed. We opened the provision box, gathered wood for a fire, and lying down on the grass, waited for the boys and horses. Here we all enjoyed a late and welcome breakfast, supplemented by small ripe strawberries which were abundant. Our return was uneventful, and we reached Elk Park before sunset. The air was balmy, the sky full of golden edged clouds. Neither sight nor sound of a mosquito, the sometimes only torment of the National Park, annoyed us. So we sat on a log outside the tent and supped with genuine out of doors appetite. The Gibbon [River] danced and sang close by our tent, which enclosed a group of meadow flowers in one cor-

46. This is probably Bath Lake. In the early days, bathing was permitted in the park. This particular location became a very popular spot for swimming because it was easily accessible yet secluded enough for privacy. This lake went dry in 1926, but in 1959 the Yellowstone earthquake caused it to fill again. By 1984, however, it was once again dry and has remained so to this day.

Bath Lake, 1884.
F. Jay Haynes. Montana Historical Society.

ner. I placed a buffalo's skull, white and entire, horns down,—for a candlestick, superseding the ugly bottle.

As we spread our blankets a fearful chorus of guttural howls and yelps arose in our vicinity. "A pack of wolves is coming down on our fold," I thought, and crying out to Ernest and Peter, received the explanation that the "gentle voices" were those of a great multitude of cranes, who gather at the river every summer evening and report on the crop of bull frogs.[47]

On the following morning we crossed a trembling bridge of pine poles and followed a steep blazed trail up the mountain side to the Monument Geysers, a long mile distant.[48] They are a very strange group, rising from a narrow strip of white lime. The bed of a once

47. Wolves lived in and around Yellowstone National Park at the time of Mary Richards's visit. However, by 1926 the Yellowstone wolf population was eliminated after several years of extermination efforts. There have been scattered sightings reported since 1926 but none have been officially confirmed, and the presence of wolves is a matter of speculation. Currently under way is the approval process for a plan by the U.S. Fish and Wildlife Service to reintroduce wolves into Yellowstone National Park and the northern Rockies.

For a discussion of the disappearance of wolves from Yellowstone National Park see Alston Chase, *Playing God in Yellowstone* (Boston: The Atlantic Monthly Press, 1986), 119–41. Also, for an overview of the history of general wildlife policy in Yellowstone see Richard A. Bartlett, *Yellowstone: A Wilderness Besieged* (Tucson: University of Arizona Press, 1985), 327–45. An essay on the difficulties relating to efforts to reintroduce wolves to the northern Rockies is Rick Bass, *The Ninemile Wolves* (Livingston: Clark City Press, 1992). See also U.S. Fish and Wildlife Service, *Northern Rocky Mountain Wolf Recovery Plan* (Denver: U.S. Fish and Wildlife Service, 1987).

48. At one time, Monument Geyser Basin was a favorite attraction owing to its strange tombstone-like cones. Today it can be reached by hiking the same "long mile." Its trailhead is in Gibbon Canyon, five miles south of Norris Basin. Monument Geyser has a small spray of erupting water, but other nearby cones are now dormant.

great stream extends to the Park below. The geysers seem to have outgrown the period of constant spouting and boiling, and merely grumble and simmer at the surface.

There were no signs of recent eruptions of water; the plateau and stream bed being comparatively dry and cool. We noticed a few perforations and crevices from which steam issued at intervals. The "Monuments" are five in number. The most conspicuous is a petrified tree trunk, three feet in diameter at its base, and five feet high. It is white and hard as marble, and sends up through its hollow center, a straight, slender column of swift moving, scalding steam.

The remaining four form a curious group at a short distance, resembling a rough cut family of tigers:—one couchant, one on the qui-vive, and a rolled up cub playing at the foot of the keeper, he being a plump, short fellow leaning over his dangerous pets. The watching tiger has an orifice in his head, just in easy reach of one's eye or ear. To apply either is venturesome. An invisible current of hot air escapes this marble throat and the growling of a discontented spirit down below is plainly heard. This, however, was a very mild geyser field at the time of our visit. The most timid could study closely its objects without fear, save perhaps that of a burned face or finger.

Two miles from this place, on the other side of the river we found the "Devil's Paint Pots,"[49] and a very ex-

49. The "Devil's Paint Pots" Richards refers to are actually on Paintpot Hill, which is located at the north end of Gibbon Canyon. Its elevation is 8,055 feet. In 1885 Charles Whitmell reported:

tensive collection of colors they hold. These "Pots," rocky bowls of varied dimensions, are sunken near each other on a hillside. Their contents resemble freshly mixed paint, each bowl containing a different color. Among the above there are pools of clear water; all are boiling furiously, and the overflow of water "paint" flows rapidly down the slope to the Park level and Geyser Creek.

As we came in sight of our first Park halting ground an unexpected scene presented itself. The lawn we left a solitude was [now] dotted with tents. Hundreds of horses and mules were grazing, drinking or prospecting on the steep hillsides; scores of heavy wagons and long lines of emptied pack saddles were placed on the left bank of the stream, and the smoke of many and scattered camp fires rose from where groups of men sat or lay on the grass.

All this we saw, and felt a regret that the peace of our first home in the Park, had departed, that we were no longer "monarchs of all we surveyed." We learned that the assemblage was a government surveying party, including an astronomer, who is to verify certain territorial division lines. This very civil party has a large military escort, and is both marking and making new roads. The location and use of said roads deponent is unable to ascertain.

"Emerging from the Cañon into meadow land, we dismount and make our way on foot through the forest to the Gibbon Paint Pots, a very curious place. The springs are small, but numerous, and contain boiling mud of various colors; white, orange, red, green, etc." (Whitmell, "The American Wonderland," 94.)

Our journey to-day has been a short one of only six-teen miles. The way seems rougher on our return for we knew its ups and downs, and could not look forward hopefully to a smoother rod of its distance. We believe a degree of military discipline prevails outside, for as we write, the notes of a bugle ring out clearly under the starry sky. The echo of Geyserland replies its call, what-ever it may be. To me it says "all is well."

The Yellowstone River in Hayden Valley, 1881.
F. Jay Haynes. Montana Historical Society.

❧ Indescribable Beauties

*A New Trail. Bruin Follows the Wagon. Sulphur
Mountains. Camping in the Wilderness. Fellow Campers Bake and Burn Their Bread.*

BANKS OF THE YELLOWSTONE RIVER,
TUESDAY EVENING, AUGUST 8.

May you live to visit, enjoy, and remember
the Yellowstone National Park. I dip my
pen in ink to-night with a keen sense of the audacity of
an effort to continue my feeble description of its beau-
ties. We are located for the night on a grass hill rising
from the inner bend of a sharp angle in the longed-for
river, which, having left the lake fifteen miles above and
intervening hills and valleys, enters at this sudden turning, deeper and narrowing channels leading into the
thick forest.

Except southward, where a grassy meadow like a
gateway opens on this paradise, we are surrounded by
hills and distant mountains, which on the east, north,

67

and west, rise to a great height of ten to twelve thousand feet. Purple, misty looking cliffs, interlocked like clasped finger[s], inclose the Rapids, the Falls, and Great Canyon of the Yellowstone. The wagon road terminates at this point; at times to-day it has been nearly impracticable.

A small company of workmen, whose tents and horses are below us on the edge of the stream, are opening a new road below the foot-trail.[50] In future seasons, visitors to the canyon may view it from a wagon seat. Our path for to-morrow's walk is visible, leading over the near grassy hills and into the thick pine forest.

At sunrise this morning we forded for the fifth time the Fire Hole River, leaving a Chinaman servant at the log hotel the only visible awake creature in the Basin. Tents were all closed, not a fire lighted; even the horses and mules stood or layed motionless in the grass.

We find by experience that a long nooning agrees with both man and beast, hence these very early startings. Turning eastward from the Mammoth Hot Springs road, we entered on one untried, leading to the Lake Falls and Canyon. It proved a shade better, the soil

50. This was part of the effort to improve the roads throughout the park by removing rocks and stumps, building bridges, and easing grades. In his annual report for 1882, Patrick Conger stated, "The rest of the men, under Captain Topping, continued work on the road. I directed them first to go over the road to the Yellowstone Lake, a distance of 35 miles from this point, and put the same in good repair, and then turned their attention toward the Great Falls and the Grand Cañon of the Yellowstone." Patrick H. Conger, *Annual Report of the Superintendent of the Yellowstone National Park to the Secretary of the Interior* (Washington: Government Printing Office, 1882), 6.

being at times gravelly and the stumps more accommo-
dating. Ascending and fording were the order of to-day. The East Fork of Fire Hole Basin River crossed our path
five times.[51]

While walking a few rods in advance of the wagon
we came upon a last night's camp by Mary's Lake.[52] On
the soft, moist sand we discovered tracks of two bears
differing much in size. We have been favored by long or
short range interviews with members of all the known
families inhabiting the woods and waters of the Park,
save that of Mr. Bruin. We hope, however, to salute a
young and small bear before we leave the region favored
by his presence. We learn that at nightfall he follows the
track of wagons, horses or men, visiting their deserted
camp fires and gaining his summer livelihood by appro-
priating all eatables left. Here allow me to state the fact
that the cook of our expedition, and probably his broth-
erhood of the frontier, look upon cold food of any description as unfit for the human stomach. Hence our
daily meals have been served literally "hot as fire,"

. This trail ran alongside what is now Nez Perce Creek to Mary
Lake, past Sulphur Mountain, and then into Hayden Valley. One can
experience this route by hiking the Nez Perce Trail and the Mary
Mountain Trail. See Orville Bach, Jr., *Exploring the Yellowstone Back-
country* (San Francisco: Sierra Club Books, 1991).

52. Mary Lake is ten miles east of the junction of the Firehole
River and Nez Perce Creek. According to Edwin Stanley, who was
journeying through Yellowstone in 1873, the lake got its name when
"on its pebbly shore some members of our party unfurled the Stars
and Stripes, and christened it Mary's Lake, in honor of Miss Clark, a
young lady belonging to our party." Edwin J. Stanley, *Rambles in
Wonderland: Or Up the Yellowstone and Among the Geysers and Other Curiosities of the National Park* (New York: D. Appleton and Co., 1878),
123.

A tourist party on the Hayden Valley Road at Sulfur Mountain, 1885.
Yellowstone National Park Archives.

hence also the bear attached to our train has been well supplied with plump, white biscuit, delicate slices of browned ham, and we presume, has examined, perhaps tasted and approved, the contents of half-emptied cans of jellies, fruits, milk and salmon. Nothing is wasted.

This afternoon we passed closely by the "Sulphur Mountains"; two enormous hills, one hundred feet high rising abruptly from a white plateau, and entirely destitute of vegetation.[53] These strange hills furnish the specimen seeker with choice flakes and blocks of alum and powders, rolls and crystals of sulphur, which collect in purest quality and unlimited quantity around and above boiling pits at their base.

We have no room for loneliness to-night. Another wagon stands near ours, two black mules graze with our horses and a second white tent stands out in bold relief against the pine forest. Two men and a dog have come to hunt and fish a week in the vicinity. They are novices in outdoor life. The first article unshipped was a sheet-iron cook stove. This they soon had red hot with a diet of pine cones. After stirring flour and other material in an iron pan, they placed it in the oven, recrammed the stove with fuel and went down the river bank to chat with the workmen, and afterwards for a bath. As I write, the odor of burning biscuit and fumes of blazing pitch reach my wagon seat, and call my attention from these pages. Poor boys! They will ask for bread and re-

53. Sulphur Mountain is located in Hayden Valley between Alum Creek to the north and Trout Creek to the south. Its elevation is 7,937 feet, and it is an area of extensive sulphur activity.

ceive only cinders on their return. One comforting as-
surance I find for them, they will live and learn. They
shall receive the bear's bread ration to-night.

🐦 Yellowstone Canyon

A Glorious Tramp from Breakfast to Dinner. Lookout Point. The Eagle's Nest. Falls And Rapids of the Yellowstone.

YELLOWSTONE RIVER,
WEDNESDAY, EVENING, AUG. 9.

An easy trail of three miles leads through the forests to Lookout Point, passing on the way the Rapids, the upper and the lower, or Great Falls of the Yellowstone. To go and return between breakfast and dinner time is a pleasant walk, which any well woman should be able to accomplish and enjoy. We took staff and sketch book, and started soon after breakfast, across the still dewy grass of the hillside.

The path through the forest and by the river bank has no peculiar charm save its solitude. Whether winding among tall trees, around frowning cliffs, rising to a hill top, or skirting the steep bank, you perceive no token of human existence, you gain no glimpse of habitation,

Yellowstone River above the Falls, 1881.
F. Jay Haynes. Montana Historical Society.

vehicle, boat or sign board. Not even a log is felled for a bridge over the sometimes deep brooks to the river. The narrow trail beneath your feet, bearing faint impress here and there of foot prints, is the sole witness that you are not the Adam or Eve of pedestrians to this wilderness of beauty.

The Rapids are soon reached. They roar and tumble over the boulders lying at the base of converging precipices for a quarter of a mile, then plunge in one vast white mass to a cavernous basin one hundred and forty feet below. Following the verge of the descent, we gained a footing at the first bend of the then quiet river, and engaged a charming view of the Rapids, the upper Falls and the interlying foothills beyond.

Leaving this, our first resting place reluctantly, we regained the trail and walked on listening, as the sound of the Upper grew fainter, for the voice of the "Lower Fall," one-half mile below. We often lost sight of the river, but at length, after a severe scramble down a long, steep hillside, the sound and sight of the Great Falls of the Yellowstone came to us at once. Here the conviction came to us of hopeless inability to convey in words or skilfully drawn color, any idea of the sublime terror of this fall and surrounding walls and canyon.

The river, suddenly compressed by projecting rock from a width of one hundred yards to as many feet, leaps in a mass of broken, wavering lines and columns into the vast basin three hundred and ninety-seven feet below.[54] The roar of contact with air and rock is fearful;

54. The Lower Fall of the Yellowstone River plunges a distance of 308 feet.

The rapids above the Upper Falls of the Yellowstone River, 1884.
Charles R. Savage. LDS Church Archives.

Lower Falls of the Yellowstone River, 1882.
F. Jay Haynes. Montana Historical Society.

so is the glance you send down, down the foaming terror, as you stand grasping the slight railing fixed on the over-hanging rock, which vibrates beneath your feet.

A constant cyclone of disturbed air moves about the great spray cloud at the base of the fall; the concave sides of the basin, the perpendicular walls of the near heights are forever wet and dripping with condensed mist. They fairly glow in the sunlight with color which is reflected in the falling water. The ordeal passed, each pale drop of the Yellowstone emerges from beneath an enormous mass of spray, and taking its own little place helps reform the broken ranks and marches onward through the canyon.

Lookout Point crowns one of the elevations on the left wall.[55] We there waited vainly for our boys to overtake us, and climbed to a more elevated position on a cliff less than a mile below. We were fully rewarded for our labor. We stood at least fifteen hundred feet above the river, which looked to us a mere narrow ribbon of liquid emerald. Our view extended up the canyon to the

55. This is the same Lookout Point that is visited today. It was sometimes called Point Lookout, Lookout Rock, Mount Lookout, and Prospect Point.

In 1883 Mormon Apostle Moses Thatcher visited the Grand Canyon of the Yellowstone and felt the ethereal bliss that overtook many visitors upon viewing the waterfall: "With a sigh we clambered up the rugged path, followed the trail through the pines and viewed the falls from Prospect Point. What a marvelous sight! How wonderfully grand! Man is but a mote in the midst of this mighty combination. In the deep tones of falling waters a mile away, in the rushing torrent a thousand feet below; in the sighing of winds among the pine leaves above, voiceful nature speaks of grandeur and of God." Moses Thatcher, "Falls of the Yellowstone," *The Contributor* (January 1884): 142.

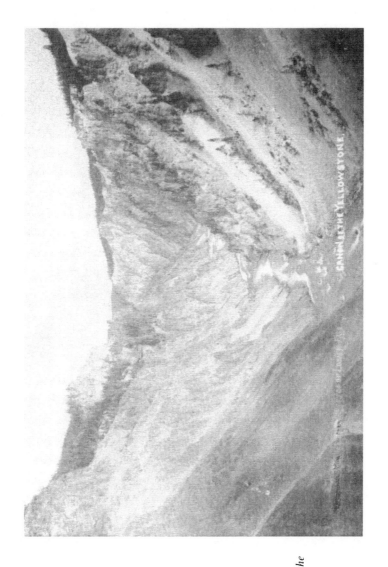

The Grand Canyon of the
Yellowstone, 1884.
Charles R. Savage.
LDS Church Archives.

fall and far into the beyond. On turning northward, we could trace for a distance of many miles the sides of the mighty chasm and its imprisoned stream.

The Canyon of the Yellowstone is unlike anything or place we have seen on either continent. Its walls rise perpendicularly or in steep slopes, and are almost entirely destitute of vegetation. The coloring of these naked mineral stained masses, resembling castles, pyramids, towers and spires, is as varied as their form. Every color possible by mixture of primaries can be seen; brown, red, grey, and yellow predominating. From our last observation point we looked directly down into two eagles' nests; in one of these were two fledglings, feebly stretching their wings and calling the parent birds, who circled widely around. The nest was made of dry tree boughs and curved sticks placed on the tops of isolated pinnacles rising six or eight hundred feet above the bed of the river.

Many irregularly shaped masses of rock, separated from the main wall, are pure white, others of various shades of ochre hold strata or projecting bars and blocks of red or black breccia. Other columnar masses, grey, purple or golden brown, rise like symmetrical pillars, crowned with capitals beautiful as those of a temple at Philae. We saw no boulder in the bed of the stream. Volumes of water flowing for ages, have removed every obstacle and deepened and smoothed the eternal channel of the great river of "Wonderland."

At length the boys and our lunch appeared. We could not eat. There are hours when the prosaic routine of bodily life seems to vanish from our consciousness. We were "etherialized" and soared with the eagles above their glorious amphitheatre. Our return to camp and the jolting of our wagon soon "materialized" us.

❧ Two Extremes

Terror and Beauty. The Terrible Mud Volcano. The Beautiful Yellowstone Lake; Its Lovely Island and Picturesque Shores. A Deserted Cabin in the Wilderness.

YELLOWSTONE LAKE,
THURSDAY, AUG. 10.

Soon after losing sight of the Sulphur Mountains we halted suddenly before a novel and terrible spectacle. A few sunken, cone-shaped pits, puffs of steam issuing from beneath wayside rocks, a belt of light, naked soil presaged a geyser vicinity, but we were unadvised of our near proximity to the "Great Mud Volcano." A high hill had evidently been halved as straightly down to its base as if done with a huge knife. One part remained intact, the other had disappeared from human ken, leaving a semicircular pit fully fifty feet wide at the base. This hole was filled nearly to the top with dirty, bad-smelling mud, stones and tree stumps, all boiling like mad, together.

83

The half hill extant was covered with grass and flowers; a few trees near the summit stretched their green boughs over the steaming, grumbling cauldron below. The semiliquid mass had extended under the gravelly base and visibly labored for its destruction with all it upheld. As we stood trembling with fright we heard and saw fragments of the tortured earth and stone fall and sink in the horrible mass. There had evidently been a recent eruption and overflow, as the ground and bushes around were covered with the same "dismal" colored mud.[56]

We declined visiting a "Devil's Den," number two of the Park, said to be a half mile west of the volcano, contenting ourselves with the interview held with "Den Number One," in the canyon of the Gibbon, last week. The remainder of our afternoon's journey was over and around hills, covered with forests of pines and skirting the river.

"Yellowstone Lake" has an altitude of 7,788 feet. Its greatest direct length is thirty, its width from ten to twenty miles.[57] Viewed from the summit of either of the three giants of its encircling mountain ranges, it resembles in shape a great silver hand with its far parted fingers. Its shores and waters are as yet almost unexplored.

56. The Mud Volcano is south of Dragons Mouth Spring, just below the south end of Hayden Valley. It was named by the Washburn Expedition in 1870 because its cone shape reminded them of a volcano. Over the years this "volcano" has become flatter and lost much of its cone shape.

57. The elevation of Yellowstone Lake is 7,733 feet. It is 14 miles wide and 20 miles long.

Trout Bay, Yellowstone Lake, 1881.
F. Jay Haynes. Montana Historical Society.

To its rare visitors they present a most picturesque aspect; some of its banks rise perpendicularly and are furrowed by cataracts and rapids pouring from snow-crested mountains; others slope gently in long, pebbly beaches; others are terraced by deposits from boiling springs that flow directly into the lake.

Fire and tempests have spared the forests that clothe all the surrounding foothills. They are of a deep green color and blend imperceptibly with the blue and purple greys of lofty heights beyond. Broad bands lying vertically or horizontally, and rounded, angular, or sharply conical caps of snow can be seen in every direction on the far away mountain sides and summits. Many islands, like masses of pine trees or baskets of fairest wild flowers, seem to float on the transparent expanse of blue, which is yet unstirred by dipping oar, unfurrowed by a gliding keel. From its unexplored inlets and covers the wild goose, duck, seagull, swan and pelican sail out their young broods, and moose, elk , bear and deer, are permitted to live fearless lives and die natural deaths in regions yet untrodden by human feet.

Near our camp we found an old weather beaten log cabin. Its roof, formed years ago of pine boughs, has gathered debris of trees, winds and winter's snows, and now is a perfect bed of waving grass and blooming flowers. Swallows have colonized its doorless, windowless, floorless, interior. Sides and top are plastered with their nests. We call the birds swallows, as they resemble the New England barn swallow in every respect except color, these being of a dark velvety brown, uniform except at the neck, which has a collar the color of

Yellowstone Lake and
Mount Sheridan, 1884.
F. Jay Haynes. Montana
Historical Society.

old gold encircling it. They seemed entirely undisturbed by our presence and allowed us to examine unoccupied nests, without a twitter of remonstrance.

We are about to break camp and shall regrettingly leave this enchanting shore. The pure, exhilarating atmosphere, its savage solitude, its scenery of varied, inexhaustible beauty, have given us a season of content and rest kin to the "Peace that passeth understanding." Our morning's bath was in a shallow, white bleached cove where the water, warmed by unseen streams from hot springs, made us envy the very fishes that could breakfast as well as bathe there. We explored the shore during the afternoon for several miles above and below our camp. Scattered along the entire distance we found rare and beautiful specimens of petrified wood, variously colored quartz, obsidian, and a few fragments of azurite.

Last night's sunset seemed made for us alone. We sat on the shore in the great silence and looked on water, earth and sky, all glorious with forms and colors we had seen only in dreams. Never can we forget the setting of the day king below the majestic and lonely mountains that gird America's fairest lake.

❧ Drawing to a Close

*Hell's Half Acre. Excelsior, Sheridan and Great
Geyser. Mule Consumes a Towel. More Friends.*

UPPER GEYSER BASIN,
SATURDAY, AUG. 12, 1882.

Tourists to "Wonderland" in near future seasons can and will dispense with camping outfit. They will "do" the tour in far less time in city
clothes. The modern Hotel Fiend is now legally let loose
by Uncle Sam in my arcadia. I know full well the followers in his train. Palatial cars will bear the traveler to
the edge of the Park, where fences, toll houses, nurseries, malarias, regulations and high prices will begin.
The "Paint Pots" and "Sulphur Mountains" may be
sold to stock companies for utilization and Falls and
Geysers can be set to work running elevators, heating
apartments and cooking the food of mammoth hotels.

89

The tent will be folded and laid away and the camp fire

extinguished.

How great has been our privilege to follow so closely the trail of the Indian and the pioneer. We met a very unique family party on our way hither. A father, mother, daughter, and son, each mounted on a mare followed by her colt, and as rear guard, a big dog followed by a small one. The party proceeded in single file in the order enumerated, even when fording the river; the colts and dogs swimming without breaking rank. The children were quite young, but brave, rosy and happy as larks. We learned that they lived on a ranch in Montana. They had not even a tent for shelter; their blankets and provisions were compactly packed and each mare carried part.

The Midway Geyser Basin is but four miles from Marshall's log hotel. Here is the largest hot spring, and the geyser throwing the greatest volume of water in the known world. "Hell's half acre" is the name universally accepted on the spot. We found it awful as its name. It includes three pools of boiling water in a state of constant overflow and the immense geyser known as the "Great," the "Excelsior," or the "Sheridan." A "Tourist's Road," designated by a sign board, leads directly down into a swiftly flowing and deep river, which at the time of our crossing was changed in color and much increased in volume by cataracts pouring over the opposite bank for a space of fifty or sixty yards. The terrors of the Half acre were hidden by dense clouds of spray and steam. Dismounting from our dripping wagon we walked over a narrow, treacherous looking road around

*Hell's Half Acre (Midway
Geyser Basin) and the
Firehole River, 1884.
F. Jay Haynes. Montana
Historical Society.*

The Excelsior Geyser, Midway Geyser Basin, 1888.
F. Jay Haynes. Montana Historical Society.

three vast pools filled to their brims with boiling water. On each side as you look at the other, you tremble to realize how fragile is the crust on which you just stood. The eye cannot measure the depth of these cavities, but their incurved sides are like intricate carvings of translucent marble. All these pools have paroxysms of boiling and overflow; but the Excelsior, which previous to the spring of 1879, presented the same characteristics, then became suddenly the enormous intermittent, spouting geyser it now is. The interval between its eruptions is not yet determined. [58]

The Excelsior has an aperture of oval shape, two hundred and fifty [feet] long by one hundred and eighty feet

58. As Old Faithful is today, the Excelsior was the "must see" geyser from 1880 to 1888. Unlike Old Faithful, it was not predictable. It was, however, enormous: the crater was 276 feet by 132 feet, its eruptions were some 300 feet high and 300 feet wide. An enthusiastic writer in 1884 declared: "We now come to the Excelsior Geyser, which is doubtless the most powerful geyser known in the world. . . . It is a sufficiently awe-inspiring experience to stand at the verge of this steaming lake, upon the hollow crust which projects over the boiling water, and peer down upon the agitated surface as the clouds of scalding vapor are occasionally lifted by the breeze. But when the geyser is in action, the awful noise and concussion produced by the falling water, accompanied by rumblings and vibrations like those of an earthquake, and the disagreeable habit of vomiting up stones, which is a special characteristic, warrant the visitor in keeping a safe distance away during the display of its terrible power." De Vallibus, "Wonders of the Yellowstone," *The Contributor* (October 1884): 87–88.

Its last eruption was in 1888, although the Excelsior unexpectedly showed some commotion in 1891 and in 1901. For the next 84 years it lay dormant; until in 1985 it showed mild activity with a small eruption of half a dozen feet. See Lee Whittlesey, "Monarch of All These Mighty Wonders: Tourists and Yellowstone's Excelsior Geyser, 1881–1890," *Montana: The Magazine of Western History* (Spring 1990): 2–15.

wide; its walls are nearly perpendicular and their depth varies from twenty to forty feet. We had arrived just at the close of a great performance and the water was sinking rapidly with a terrific gurgling into the unfathomable throats or chimneys of the basin. In few moments the very last drop disappeared, steam ceased to ascend and all became quiet as if the giant below slept to gather strength for another outbreak. The situation, though interesting, was far from comfortable, and with steam soaked garments and wet, hot boots, we recrossed the river, regained the road and proceeded on our rough way,—walking the remaining five miles to the place from which I write. We found at every rod of the path some unique object or some picturesque view. The wonders of the Upper Basin, scarcely three miles square, are unrivalled. Fuel and pure water are comparatively scarce and the selection of our camping ground was not unanimously made.

Although the Fire Hole Basin river flows through this heated valley, it receives all the overflow of at least a thousand boiling pools and geysers; any one of the latter exceeding in its daily or hourly outpour any artificial fountain that rises to beautify our cities at man's bidding. Our tent is near the river on a small grassy knoll. Directly between us and the stream is a noisy little fountain which we have named "Ours." It boils up from its central bowl for just twenty minutes, then throws up a single jet which falls separated in a thousand lines of gems and rainbows. The sight of this little object alone compensates for the fatigue of many a long walk. When the breeze arose at eventide its warm spray was wafted even within our tent. We have also a natural laundry near by, furnished with stone tubs into which the water flows clear and sufficiently cool for use. The boys have succeeded in washing therein our camp linen and tins till they have the color of snow and silver.

A ludicrous incident has just occurred. A stray mule from another camp has eaten one towel and was caught in the act of swallowing a fragment of a second. We are not alone in this strange, weird region. Other tents are stationed wherever a bit of grassy meadow, or a green knoll, once a geyser cone, rises from the barren, silicious sources of ever flowing brooks.

❧ Last Sunday in Camp

Watching the Great Spouters. Two Eruptions in
Twenty-four Hours of the Grand Geyser of the World.
Returning to Civilization. Departure from the Park.

UPPER GEYSER BASIN,
SUNDAY, AUG. 13.

It is the Sabbath day. Everything around us
seems to move. There is a strong breeze blow-
ing from the south, the river flows noisily over its
rocky bed, several of the big fountains of the basin are in
full play, and from our position four are visible. We
scarcely know where to allow our eyes to linger. By
walking less than [a] quarter of a mile, we can stand
close beside, climb upon, or look straight down the
throats of five unrivalled geysers. There are literally
hundreds of "Spouters" in full view.

The "Castle, Giant, Beehive, Saw Mill, Grotto,
T'an[59] and the Grand" have each given a magnificent ex-

59. "T'an" *may* be the Turban geyser. Reau Campbell's 1923

97

hibition within the past twenty-four hours. The Giantess and Willow are yet waited for. The frequency and duration of the eruptions and the height of the column or jet thrown up by the ten chief geysers has been determined with tolerable accuracy. The Castle seems to us most imposing in form, the Grotto most beautiful, but Old Faithful is the most punctual in his appearance. The throats of the "T'an" diverging in a straight line from a central chimney explain the peculiar shape its jets present. This geyser is the first that the traveler sees of the celebrated ten of the Basin. The Beehive has precisely the form of an old style straw hive; it stands on a perfectly flat, barren white "half acre," and as it is not over four feet high its single chimney can be very easily "looked into." This is a very beautiful geyser, rising once in twenty-four hours, in a single jet two feet in diameter at its base. Frequent puffings of steam and severe rumblings precede its eruption, and those who wait near this or others of its kin, must take warning, and flee with all speed, or bear, perhaps, the fatal result of a douche of scalding water falling from the great height of two hundred and twenty feet.

The columnar masses of water rising at intervals from the vertical or sinuous chimneys of the Castle and the Grotto are wonderfully picturesque. Their principal

---

guide stated that the "Turban plays with a frequency that is gratifying, and when the eruption occurs simultaneously with the Grand, which it often does, the effect is fine." Reau Campbell, *Complete Guide and Descriptive Book of the Yellowstone* (Chicago: E. M. Campbell, 1923), 114.

The cone of the Castle Geyser, Upper Geyser Basin, n.d. F. Jay Haynes. LDS Church Archives.

*Grotto Geyser, Upper
Geyser Basin, 1884.
Charles R. Savage.
LDS Church Archives.*

*Visitors at Old Faithful,
ca. 1876.
Charles R. Savage.
LDS Church Archives.*

orifices are from three to five feet in diameter, sending up columns from fifty to one hundred feet; but from other lesser throats within and around the milk-white edifices, a hundred smaller jets arise, all playing together from twenty to thirty minutes. The effect of these swift-moving waters, in bright sunlight and clad in many rainbows, towards the blue sky and afterwards breaking in a gem-like shower on marble-like domes, walls and terraces beneath, is a scene of rare splendor. "Old Faithful" is the soul of punctuality. He is a favorite with all whose hours here are limited. Every sixty-seven seconds [minutes] the year round, he throws up a column of water six feet in diameter at the base, to the height of two hundred feet. The cone of this great geyser is somewhat flattened and affords excellent footing to those who care to inspect nearly the home of the only spouter who never changes his habits.

We have been doubly favored within twenty-four hours by two displays of the "Grand Geyser of the World," so called by scientists. A foot bridge spans the river and on the summit of a little ridge lying close to the green foothills is the twenty by twenty-five foot bowl from which rises at intervals not yet determined, the most enormous, the grandest of grand fountains. Two Bostonians left camp yesterday, after waiting three days in vain for the sight we have enjoyed twice within the twenty-four hours following their departure. They will set down this fountain in their records as untrustworthy, and with reason.

The waters of the Saw Mill, Giantess and Grand have built no edifice above the surface. They rise from basins,

Beehive Geyser in the Upper Geyser Basin, 1882.
F. Jay Haynes. Montana Historical Society.

Giant Geyser, Upper Geyser Basin, ca. 1886. Note the people standing on the cone during the eruption. F. Jay Haynes. LDS Church Archives.

or from pools, quiet and peaceful looking enough till within a few moments before an eruption. Then sub- teranean noises increase, steam issues at short intervals and the "Safety valve" or "Indicators" near begin to emit jets of hot water. The basin fills or the pool over- flows and suddenly, with a noise "harder" than thun- der, the immense column shoots up into the sky as if it would actually vanish from sight in the blue depths above. The Grand throws its mighty column to the known height of four hundred feet, and almost un- brokenly for half the distance, when it parts and hun- dreds of gracefully curved jets spread still upward, for a few seconds lingering there and then breaking like shat- tered atoms of heaven's pearly gates turning to ashy dross as earth is touched. We all gazed spell-bound at this glorious spectacle, which was repeated six times at intervals of two minutes. I was conscious that the lady by my side was timing the eruptions by her watch.

The next forenoon at eleven o'clock as we were seated watching for the Beehive's debut we heard Ernest shout "There goes the Indicator!" and all started at full speed for the vicinity of the Grand, about an eighth of a mile distant. Mrs. F. and M. B. R. never need be ex- pected to make better time than they did on that unex- pected occasion. We were fully recompensed for our pains, and stood short-breathed and weary, with a score of other fortunates, at the foot of the Grand, where the spectacle of the preceding afternoon was repeated. Would that we could divide our remembrance with the disappointed Boston pilgrims.

To-morrow we commence our return journey to

Beaver Canyon and the semi–civilized life of the frontier of Idaho and Wyoming. We leave some interesting localities unvisited; and hope another season to explore Lower Creek and Falls, the region around the Snowy and Specimen Mountains and eastern shores of the Yellowstone Lake. We leave with genuine regret the National Park; where, added to the charm of its delicious air, the grandeur of its mountains and waterfalls, and the unique beauty of its geyser scenery, we have found the joy of absence from the "vanities and cares that wither life and waste its little hour."

ACKNOWLEDGMENTS

The more experience I gain in life, the more I realize that nothing is accomplished without the assistance of others. With that idea in mind, I wish to express my gratitude to the people whose names follow (in no particular order).

I appreciate the help of the staff of the Essex Institute of Salem, Massachusetts, especially Director William LaMoy and Reference Librarian Nancy Heywood. Thanks to my wife, Sheri Eardley Slaughter, and my friend Jay Burrup for their help and advice on genealogical research. Steve Ives, Llewellyn Howland, and Robert Weir were very helpful with their suggestions and efforts. Tom Tankersley, the Archivist and Historian of Yellowstone National Park, and Elsa Kortge, the photo curator of Yellowstone, were always willing and able to help at a moment's notice. The Photograph Archivist of the Montana State Historical

Society, Rebecca Kohl, and Bennie Morgan were more than helpful in my efforts to locate photographs from the Haynes Photograph Collection. I am grateful to Judith Austin of the Idaho State Historical Society. The criticisms and urgings of Will Bagley were very beneficial. My daughter, Danielle Slaughter, was indispensable in all of the many tasks she willingly performed. Thanks to Tom Child for the map. Ronald O. Barney deserves some kind of award for listening to me and continually encouraging me on this project. Wesley Slaughter, my son, was supportive throughout this project and, like his sister, has always shown an interest in and a love of Yellowstone. I am greatly indebted to Jeff Grathwohl, Associate Director of the University of Utah Press, who was always interested, patient, and constructive. If there is anyone I have forgotten, please forgive me.

William W. Slaughter

William W. Slaughter is a photo archivist for the Historical Department Archives of the Church of Jesus Christ of Latter-Day Saints in Salt Lake City. He enjoys hiking, observing wildlife, camping, and skiing.